The Discovery of America & Other Myths

The meeting of two worlds across the bridge of language: the translator La Malinche as intermediary between the Aztecs and the Spaniards. (16ᵗʰ c.)

The Discovery of America & Other Myths

A NEW WORLD READER

■■■■

Thomas Christensen and Carol Christensen, editors

Chronicle Books San Francisco

Pages 245-246 constitute a continuation of the copyright page.

Printed in the United States of America.

Library of Congress Cataloging-in-Publication Data

The discovery of America & other myths: a new world reader / Thomas Christensen and Carol Christensen, editors
    p. cm.
  Includes bibliographical references and index.
  ISBN 0-8118-0186-1
    1. Columbus, Christopher—Influence. 2. America—Discovery and exploration—Spanish. 3. Indians—First contact with Western civilization. I. Christensen, Thomas, 1948-   . II. Christensen, Carol, 1947-   . III. Title: Discovery of America and other myths.
E111.D63 1992   92-3955
970.01'5—dc20   CIP

Cover design: Julie Noyes Long
Book design: Peter Rutledge Koch
Composition: Ann Flanagan Typography
Cover image: Neil Shigley

Distributed in Canada by Raincoast Books,
112 East Third Avenue, Vancouver, B.C. V5T 1C8

10 9 8 7 6 5 4 3 2 1

CHRONICLE BOOKS
275 Fifth Street
San Francisco, CA 94103

for Guy Davenport

CONTENTS

FOREWORD

Waiting for Columbus

by

Alastair Reid

For some time now, I have viewed the coming of 1992 with a certain dread. It can hardly have escaped anyone's attention that on October 12th five hundred years will have passed since Christopher Columbus first stepped ashore on what was for him a new world, however ancient its inhabitants. From the vantage point of Europe, he began to make a vast unknown into a known, and the date has been nailed down in history as that of the discovery of America. Not surprisingly, 1992 has been steadily in the sights of many quickening interests, public and private, and countless plans have been laid to turn the year into a circus of near-global celebration. It is understandable that governments should seize on such occasions for a bit of national brio, the satisfaction of having come a long way. It puts some kind of affirmative stamp on a doubtful present; and, besides that, it gives the year a "theme," which can be echoed inexhaustibly in exploitable form. The year 1992 is a prospective gold mine: the books, bumper issues of magazines, television specials, documentaries, simulations, and reenactments, and the coins, medallions, ship models, maps, museum exhibits, and other icons, yet unimaginable. One Spanish sculptor, Antoni Miralda, set in motion plans for a symbolic marriage between the Statue of Liberty and the statue of Columbus that stands on a cast-iron column overlooking the harbor of Barcelona. Outsized wedding garments and jewelry have already been on display in various capital cities, and the symbolic ceremony was held on St. Valentine's Day in Las Vegas. It occurs to me that if only Columbus had had the foresight to acquire the fifteenth-century equivalent of an agent his descendants would be raking in much more gold this year than even the Admiral dreamed of amassing, abundant though these dreams were, during his various sallies westward.

Of the thirty-odd countries that have pledged themselves to official quincentenary fervor, Spain is outdoing all the others in extravagance, spending hundreds of millions of dollars on the event. Spain, after all, made the initial investment in the Admiral's enterprise, and it is clearly looking to 1992 as a way of reaping even more than it already has from that first outlay. This year, Spain is the setting for a World's Fair (in Seville) and for the Olympic Games (in Barcelona), and Madrid has been named Europe's City of Culture for the year. All these events are expected to attract a vast intrusion of tourists—tourism being an industry that Spain has been turning to great advantage since the sixties. Spain is ripe for a year of self-congratulation: since the death of Francisco Franco, in 1975, it has made itself into a responsible and sophisticated modern democracy, an active and energetic member of the European Community, with a new and zippy life style and an aggressive self-confidence. Spain has been trumpeting the quincentenary: in 1988, the Spanish government established a foundation in Washington, D.C.— SPAIN '92—"to engage Americans in a thoughtful exploration of the impact of Christopher Columbus' voyages and to strengthen the cultural traditions which unite Americans and Spaniards," in the words of its brochure. Spain has also had built meticulous replicas of the three ships that made the first voyage—the Santa María of a design the Spanish called a *nao*, slower and statelier than the caravels Niña and Pinta. They were launched by members of the Spanish Royal Family in the fall of 1989, and set sail in a reenactment of the voyage. Now they are showing themselves around the Caribbean before turning up to lead the tall ships into New York Harbor this Fourth of July. They are not, however, the only replicas of that little fleet; several have been built—enough to stage a round-the-world caravel race if they are all still afloat after their strenuous year of simulation. One replica of the Santa María has been built in Barcelona by a Japanese publisher, who intends to sail it all the way from Barcelona to Kobe, Japan, thus fulfilling Columbus's original plan, which was to find the trade route from Spain to the lucrative East.

Ever since the quincentenary loomed, however, there has arisen a countercry, close to an outcry, over the global fiesta, and it has mostly come, understandably, from the countries of Spanish America—the discoverees, as it were, which were of course given no choice about being discovered. What came to these countries with the conquest was nothing good—violent invasion, massacre, enslavement, exploitation—and a number of voices have strongly suggested that 1992 be observed as a year of mourning in Spanish America and the Caribbean. Cuba has been scathing in its denunciations of the celebrations. I was sent a copy of the "Declaration of Mexico," circulated by a group for the "Emancipation and Identity of Latin America." To give the declaration's gist, I quote its first and last articles:

> Whereas October 12, 1492, which according to a Eurocentric version of history was the "discovery" and / or "encounter between two worlds," marked the beginning of one of the greatest acts of genocide, pillage, and plunder in human history, and whereas the intention to celebrate its 500th Anniversary constitutes an act of arrogance and disdain for the peoples of the Third World . . .

> . . . we have resolved not to participate in any activity related to the official celebrations of the 500th Anniversary, since such participation would legitimize the historical system of injustice and dependence initiated on October 12, 1492, and the spurious character of its celebration.

Rumblings from Latin America notwithstanding, the country that has dressed the coming quincentenary in the most official pomp and gravity has been the Dominican Republic, which, with Haiti, occupies the island Columbus christened Hispaniola—the first whole territory subdued and settled by the fortune hunters from Spain. Santo Domingo, the present-day capital, was the first outpost, the first colonial city in the New World, and its cathedral contains at least some of the Admiral's remains. (Havana and Seville claim to have the other parts in their keeping.) For the country's President, Dr. Joaquín Balaguer, who is eighty-four, the quincentenary has been an obsession from an early age, and his long life seems to have been single-mindedly aimed at October 12, 1992. As far back as 1986, Balaguer instituted the Permanent Dominican Commission for the Fifth Centenary of the Discovery and Evangelization of America—the longest and most pompous banner so far flown in the name of the event. He appointed as head of the commission his close friend and ecclesiastical henchman the Archbishop of Santo Domingo, Nicolás López Rodríguez, who views the landing of Columbus as the most momentous event in Christendom since the Resurrection. Balaguer clearly expects the quincentenary to bring to his country an attention and a sense of importance until now earned only by a rich crop of exceptional baseball players. Columbus, in his "Journal of the First Voyage," speaks of the island as "the fairest ever looked on by human eyes"—an endorsement that is still used liberally by the Dominican Tourist Office.

The country certainly seemed so to me when I first went there, over ten years ago. Outside its capital and two or three lesser cities, it is rural and agricultural, dotted sparsely with small villages, outposts of subsistence, so that its beautiful and immensely varying landscapes always dominate. Dominicans are among the most cheerful people in the world, and I found myself going back to explore further. I eventually settled on the Samaná Peninsula, in the extreme northeast of the country, a narrow arm of land, thirty-two miles in length, that protrudes from the bulk of the mainland like a lobster claw into the Atlantic and forms a very long and narrow bay on its south side—a natural harbor that at different times has attracted the acquisitive attention of foreign powers, the United States among them. A low mountain spine runs along the peninsula, falling away on the north to a long sand coast and on the south to strings of beaches and small enclosed inlets. The whole peninsula is covered with coconut palms, whose easygoing crop has been for many years its principal source of revenue. Samaná is quite literally the end of the line: if you follow its single road to the tip of the peninsula, you find yourself facing a white beach, a reef, and, beyond, the open Atlantic. It was on Samaná that Columbus made his last landfall on the first voyage of discovery, and from there he set sail for Spain with news of what he had found.

It was Samaná itself, and not Columbus, that drew me in. Turns in the road revealed sudden beauties, to gasp at. Everything moved at walking pace. A car looked somehow absurd there. The place felt as if it were adrift, unanchored to anything. I explored the villages and the coast, I asked questions, I listened a lot, and eventually I acquired a piece of land just inside the point where Samaná Bay opens to the Atlantic: land that rose in a broad bowl from a small enclosed beach to a ridge, and fell away to the road on the other side; land that faced south across the bay and was thickly overgrown—well staked with coconut palms, all nodding seaward. Don Justo, who sold me the land, told me that he had not seen it in years, although he lives only a few miles from it. He had sent a man four times a year to gather the coconuts, but he did not think much else could grow there. Now he comes often, amazed that I have coaxed it into fruit.

In the Dominican countryside, campesinos live mostly in clumps of houses, settlements rather than villages—*aldea* is the Spanish word—that are dotted here and there, usually close to a water source. My land fell away steeply on the west side to a small, flat clearing through which a freshwater stream flowed by way of a small lagoon into the sea. Five houses stood close to the stream, accommodating in all about twenty people—men, women, a tribe of children. After buying the land, I made arrangements to stay in a room in one of the houses, and I hired the men of the *aldea* to help me build a small house, and to clear the land for cultivation. During that time, I got to know my neighbors very well indeed. We were some nine miles beyond the last town—that is, beyond public market, post office, electricity, telephone, hospital, and hardware store—and everybody depended on the small country *colmados*, which sold the basics: rice, oil, sugar, salt, rum. What we lived in—our bounded world—was, I learned from them, our *vecindad*, or neighborhood, which meant roughly the piece of coast you could encompass with a sweep of the arm from the ridge. Within the *vecindad*, you knew the inhabitants, down to the babies, and if you did not actually know them you had heard about them, in story form, and you inevitably shared their crises and daily dramas.

When you settle in a place, what you absorb, and to some extent take on, from those who live there is their vantage point: the way they see the rest of the world, their preoccupations, the web of their attention. Most of my neighbors are *analfabetos*; they neither read nor write. They are, however, passionate, dedicated talkers, often eloquent. Their mode, their natural wavelength, is to put themselves in story form. Their lives have no written archives, their years no numbers or dates; for that reason, a quincentenary is meaningless to them. They have saved their personal history in the form of a set of stories, well polished with telling, stored, ready. I have heard some of them recount their lives, a rosary of stories, on different occasions, and noticed how they vary with the telling. Everything that happens eventually circulates in story form, embellished by its tellers. Don León listens avidly to the radio news in his store and passes on his edited versions of it to his customers, who disperse it further on the way home. Travelling so, from teller to teller, quite ordinary happenings often turn into wonders.

In the evenings of those first days, when we had finished work and bathed and eaten, we would sit by the stream and talk as the dark came down. My neighbors were full of questions, mostly about life in the United States, which I answered with some care; and in my turn I questioned them closely about their lives and the ways of the place. We have continued so ever since. In the evenings, I hear feet on the stones of my terrace, and some-one will materialize, always with an offering—Sandro with fish, Felipe with an egg—and we will sit on the warm stone and talk. A kind of natural barter plays a large part in my neighbors' exis-tence, and, indeed, they like nothing better than a "deal," an exchange that pleases both sides. I have to remember that I am a *patrón*, a landowner, and I have to assume the role sometimes: to settle a dispute, or to come up with money for medicine—a debt that is always paid off with a day's work. Dominican society is a curious web of family connections, of debts and favors owed, of patronage and reward—a system that, while it functions well enough in remote country settlements like ours, has turned Dominican politics into a tangle of corruption. My neighbors are natural anarchists. Pucho, who has worked with me since the beginning, and now lives, with his family, on the land above mine, insists that he has no loyalties other than to what his eye encompasses, and he leaves no ground unplanted, for that is what makes unquestionable sense to him. One evening, he found, in a catalogue that had come with my mail, a rowing machine. He was delighted, for he has a long row to the reef where he goes fishing, and hates rowing; when I explained that people in cities had rowing machines in their houses to keep healthy, he looked at me pityingly.

As I discovered by the stream, history for my neighbors is mostly hearsay, vague rumblings in a dateless clutter of past, anchored by a few facts brought home from school by the chil-dren. For most of them, the past, though it has engendered their present, is an irrelevance. So at one point, for a few evenings running, I told them a fairly simplified version, though quite a detailed one, of Cristóbal Colón and the first voyage, the first landings, the coming of the Spaniards, and the subsequent enslavement of their country. I told them what I knew about the Indians—the Taínos and the Ciguayos—who when Colón arrived had been living an unvarying rural existence. They made their settlements by fresh water, close to the sea. They fished, they bartered work and harvests, they lived communally. They were also innocent of money, as my neighbors often are, though not from choice.

Some of my neighbors became quite indignant at my version of the arrival of the Spaniards, and, indeed, I did myself. Although I had read fairly extensively about the conquest, I had always done so in the historical mass, so to speak; I had never been physically close to the scene before, and I felt myself suddenly waking up to those happenings as quite easily imaginable realities. When the house was finished and the books were unpacked, I started to read that history all over again, beginning with where I was—with Columbus's landing on Samaná—and then going mostly backward, reading what I could find about the conditions of life in Hispaniola before that catastrophic disembarkation.

In early January of 1493, aboard the Niña, with the Pinta in attendance, Columbus was bowling along the north coast of Hispaniola, on an easterly course. Of all his landfalls so far, Hispaniola had proved the most rewarding. Its natives were friendly and docile, its vegetation was sumptuous, and he had found enough gold to fuel expectations of more. It would be his territory, he had decided, his base for any future exploration. Fixed firmly in his sailing mind, however, was the urge to return to Spain with all dispatch, on the first good wind. He had lost the Santa María, grounded on a coral reef on Christmas Eve, but its timbers had been used to build a small fort called La Navidad, where the Admiral left behind a garrison of thirty-nine men. The standard histories have him rounding the northeast corner of the Samaná Peninsula and deciding to make one last landfall, to take on fresh water and provisions for the return crossing, and, if possible, to careen and caulk his two remaining boats, which were taking water. According to his log entry for January 12, 1493, the two ships entered "an enormous bay three leagues wide, with a little island [*una isleta pequeñuela*], in the middle of it," and they anchored between the little island and a shallow sand beach. The following morning, the Admiral sent a boat ashore to treat with the Indians, as he had been doing with regularity over the past three months. These Indians, however, were quite different in appearance from the ones so far encountered. These wore their hair long, plaited with bird plumage, and they blackened their faces. Also, unlike most of those so far encountered, they carried arms—longbows and arrows. The crew persuaded one of them to return to the ship and talk with the Admiral. By this time, the Spaniards had most likely acquired a certain basic vocabulary, and, as usual, the Admiral questioned the man assiduously on the whereabouts of gold, and delivered an invitation to his cacique, his chief. The Indian was fed, given some trinkets, and returned by the boat's crew to his beach. On this occasion, some fifty-five Indians had gathered, and seven of the boat's crew bargained for bows and arrows, as they had been ordered. They had acquired two bows when something caused the Indians to go back to collect their arms. Leaving nothing to chance, the seven Spaniards attacked them, wounding one Indian with a sword slash in the buttocks and another in the breast with a crossbow arrow. This brief skirmish, most likely founded on a misunderstanding, has gone into the annals as the first shedding of indigenous blood in the New World—the first, faint inkling of the slaughter that was to follow. Three days later, the wind turned westerly, and, with four of the long-haired Indians added to the on-board evidence of the New World, the Niña and the Pinta put out well before dawn and set course for Spain. In his log the Admiral referred to his last anchorage as the Golfo de las Flechas, the Bay of the Arrows.

"The Journal of the First Voyage," the written source of the discovery, is a strangely diffuse document, very far from objectivity even when it is being a ship's log, for some of its landfalls are still being argued over. (There is no original of the document. The version we read is an annotated text of a fifteen-thirties edition prepared and in many instances paraphrased by a later visitor, the diligent friar Bartolomé de Las Casas, from a less than complete copy made by an errant scribe; but not even this text was known about until 1825, when it was published, circulated, studied, and, in 1828, translated into English.) Some of the journal is first person, some third person (Las Casas' paraphrase), some in the shorthand of terse nautical observation. Columbus's own observations sometimes have the true awe of a man seeing unimagined wonders for the first time, but they are interspersed with passages of self-congratulation, lavish reassurances to Their Majesties, small sermons and other bursts of missionary zeal, inflated promises of bountiful gold, and a very eccentric geography. Columbus was in his forties by then, and for the last ten years his sole preoccupation had been to persuade some rich and powerful patron to underwrite an expedition of discovery. He had presented his arguments many times—as often as possible—first to the Portuguese court and then to Their Catholic Majesties in Spain, and he had obviously made them as alluring as he could. He was familiar with Marco Polo's chronicles, and cast his own expectations in the same high tone, conjuring up a vision of a New World that, since it was so far entirely imagined, could be wondrous in every respect. He became a practiced exaggerator. He was shrewd enough to realize that he had to satisfy a multitude of interests, and his arguments were consequently many-faceted: for mercantile interests he would discover the route to the East that would open up trade with Cathay and with Cipango (Japan); for the Crown he would claim all new lands and found for Spain a colonial empire; for the Church he could promise converts, he would find the Garden of Eden; and beyond all these interests he dangled the promise of gold in abundance, at a time when Spain's treasury was exhausted. He had voiced these expectations so often that when he did find land what he looked for first was a self-justifying confirmation of them. His New World existed for him in the fiction he had made of it before he discovered it, and there was often a considerable disparity between what he found and what he said he found. After exploring the coast of Cuba, in November, he insisted, and continued to insist, that it was Cathay; yet he did not continue west. By then, from the natives he encountered he had picked up enough stories of gold so that it was fixed abidingly in the forefront of his attention. For him, the rumor of gold brought wish and reality together. Forgetting about the East, he followed the Indians' indications and turned back in the direction of Hispaniola.

Among a handful of anecdotes that Dominicans like to tell about the conquest is one that I have heard in a few variant forms. As fact it is improbable, but as essence it is peerless. It became the practice of the caciques to retreat from the arriving Spaniards, leaving placatory gifts in their path. The story has one such cacique leaving as an offering his beautiful daughter, bound to a stake, and wearing nothing but a gold ring in her nose. The Admiral, arriving at the head of his men, stops them suddenly with spread hands, gazes at the girl for a gravid minute, then points a trembling finger and asks, "Where did you get that ring?"

I keep thinking of those first encounters, particularly from the point of view of language. The Spaniards and the Indians had no language in common, and Columbus had to communicate as tourists do nowadays in markets beyond their linguistic reach—by pointing and gesticulating. While that probably served well enough to get the ships' companies food and water, to make gestures of friendship and good intentions, and even to emphasize a particular urgent interest in anything made of gold, it cannot have made possible the communication of anything abstract, like the claiming of all the Indians' lands in the name of Ferdinand and Isabella, or the fundamental tenets of the Holy Roman Church. Over various landfalls, the Spaniards probably began to assemble a sketchy vocabulary of native words, but there are signs in the journal that Columbus was prone to the affliction of beginners in any language—an overwillingness to understand. Hearsay for Columbus was whatever he thought he heard, and hearsay was the basis of his golden promises in a famous letter that he addressed to Their Majesties on the return crossing. Besides the gold and the Indians, Columbus was carrying back with him a great fund of information that he had sifted from the Indians' stories, some of it more imagined than real. "The Journal of the First Voyage" has a kind of speculative edge to it, an awe in its voice, a looking-at that before very long became a looking-for. The second voyage, from 1493 to 1496, was no longer looking for gold; it was going after it. With the second voyage, the conquest really began.

Since about the first century, Arawak Indians had been migrating north from the South American continent through the islands, and so had settled Hispaniola a good many centuries before Columbus arrived. Those island Arawak of Hispaniola are now generally referred to as Tainos, from the name for their upper class, for, although they had originally brought with them their own plants and methods of civilization, they evolved a way of life distinct to the island. What we know of their mode of existence in Hispaniola has reached us mainly through the assiduousness of four chroniclers who came on subsequent voyages—Bartolomé de Las Casas, Peter Martyr, Guillermo Coma, and Gonzalo Fernández de Oviedo. Yet the more I read in the chronicles about how the Tainos lived, the more I realize that their life resembled, in most of its fundamentals, the present life of our *vecindad*. Taino artifacts are everywhere—the neighbors will bring me pieces of red pottery they come across, or an axe head, still lime-encrusted. Their life-sustaining crop was the root cassava—manioc, yuca, tapioca. It gave them bread, and they grew it in conelike mounds of earth called *conucos*. Cassava, yams, and sweet potato, along with beans, maize, peppers, and squashes, were their standard plantings, none of them at all demanding of attention or labor. They also grew cotton and tobacco and some fruit—pineapple and papaya in particular. With an abundance of fish, they were self-sufficient. A docile people, they were feudally organized under a cacique. They lived in small settlements close to fresh water, in simple houses, well roofed against the rains. Only hurricanes or droughts upset their equilibrium.

The selfsame crops are all flourishing in our *vecindad* at this moment. Pucho has a great spread of yuca growing just under the crest—a staple that feeds him year-round. Now we have additional staples—coconuts, bananas and plantains, rice, sugar, coffee, many more fruits—but the land and the fishing still provide practically all our food. Taino words are on our tongue every day—hammock, cassava, maize, tobacco, potato, canoe. Although the Taino population of Hispaniola was wiped out within thirty years of the discovery, it is as though the Tainos had left their mode of life embedded in the land, to be reenacted in a surprisingly similar form by the campesinos now. Rich soil, a benign climate, and plants of predictable yield guarantee basic survival, although today on a threadbare level. For the Tainos, however, it appears to have been an abundance, and their world was apparently both stable and peaceful. While the Tainos knew the whereabouts of gold, they made little use of it except for small ornaments. Sometimes, sitting on my terrace, I imagine what it must have been like for the Tainos, similarly perched, to see the caravels come into sight. Even today, when a boat of any size enters the bay we come out to gaze, as we do when a plane flies over.

In the letter Columbus wrote on the return crossing to Ferdinand and Isabella (it was addressed to Luis de Santangel, Crown Treasurer, for transmission to Their Catholic Majesties), he expanded on the nature of the Indians he had encountered, speaking of their timidity, their innocence, and the fact that they went unarmed and were both friendly to and fearful of the Spaniards—perfect material for conversion and for service to the Crown. He did report, however, that he had heard of an island peopled by warlike Indians, Caribs, who were known to eat human flesh, and who made sorties on the outlying islands. The details he gave of them—that they wore their hair long and carried bows and arrows—appear to have come from the confrontation and flash of force at Las Flechas. When his boat's crew told him of that encounter, he wrote of himself in the journal, on January 13, 1493, "In one way it troubled me, and in another way it did not, i.e., in that now they might be afraid of us.

Without doubt, the people here are evil, and I believe they are from the Isle of Caribe, and that they eat men. . . . If these people are not Caribes, they must at least be inhabitants of lands fronting them and have the same customs, not like the others on the other islands who are without arms and cowardly beyond reason."

When the seventeen ships of the second voyage reached their destination in Hispaniola, with a company of about fifteen hundred, some domestic animals, and a variety of seeds, plants, and provisions, the long equilibrium that the Tainos had enjoyed ended. Columbus found the fort he had left destroyed, all the men dead—they had abused the Indians and had been overcome in turn. From this point on, Columbus never hesitated to show force in all his dealings with the Indians. They were to be subdued and turned to work in finding and extracting gold, before all else. The Spaniards as yet had no substantial permanent settlement, but they set out on expeditions to the interior, to track the gold. The course of subsequent events was perhaps set from the beginning by a fatal misunderstanding. On the first voyage, Columbus read from the gesticulations of the Indians he questioned that gold existed on the island in abundant quantities, and he reported that as fact. In truth, while gold did exist in the Cibao and in other alluvial placers, it was not widespread, plentiful, or easily accessible—certainly not to any degree that would satisfy the Admiral's by now burning expectations. Yet he continued to insist that it was, and drove the Indians more and more ferociously to produce it.

It did not take long to turn the feelings of the Tainos for the Spaniards from fear to hatred: they first rose against them in early 1494, and suffered fierce retribution. When a fleet of four ships left for Spain, in February of 1495, about five hundred Indian captives were aboard; nearly half of them died on the voyage. Columbus meanwhile set about crushing Indian resistance once and for all, which he did with a formidable force of men. He eventually secured the submission of most of the caciques, established a fort in the center of the island, and then decided on the site of the new capital, Santo Domingo—at the mouth of the Ozama River, in the south. From every Indian over fourteen the Admiral demanded a tribute of a small piece of gold every three months. The caciques begged to be released from the tribute of gold, offering instead to plant a vast stretch of land expressly for feeding the Spaniards, something to them of infinitely greater worth. But the Spaniards, fired by both greed and impatience, were unrelenting.

Failure to pay tribute resulted in increasingly brutal punishment—quite often, according to Las Casas, the cutting off of the Indians' hands—until, in 1497, orders came from Spain, in the form of Letters Patent, decreeing a *repartimiento*, a sharing out, of the colony. The plan was later modified to become one of granting the settlers *encomiendas*, tracts of land to use and cultivate, along with an Indian community to do each settler's bidding, with the understanding that the *encomendero* would in time convert his Indians to Christianity. The granting of *encomiendas*, however, was less about land than about Indians: in practice, a settler would be given a whole Indian community, under its cacique, to cultivate the land, to dig for gold, to do anything at all that the master might command. Religious instruction was not uppermost in the settlers' minds. By 1500, the enslavement of the Tainos was complete. The seven years of Columbus's governorship of Hispaniola had been chaotic for the Spaniards and disastrous for the Tainos. His authority over the Spanish settlers had frayed and eroded, and the revenues he had promised the Crown had not been realized. Orders came from Spain that he was to be replaced as governor by Francisco de Bobadilla; and when Bobadilla arrived in Santo Domingo, in August of 1500, his first act was to arrest Columbus and his two brothers, Bartholomew and Diego, and send them back to Spain in chains.

Although Columbus has been mythified by history as the discoverer, he cannot be made to bear the blame for the greed and the brutality of those who came after him—men of a less visionary disposition. What set the ruthless tenor of the conquest, however, was the extravagant expectations that Columbus had created in his quest for patronage. His eagerness to confirm these expectations shows in what he chose to see on the first voyage. His later life seethed with frustration, as though he could never forgive the lands he had discovered for not giving him what they had promised, or what he had made them promise. His obsession with fulfilling the promise of abundant gold kept him from giving any thought to the territories he was meant to be governing, or maintaining any authority over the settlers. It was less the inhumanity of the settlers—although Las Casas has left us plenty of evidence of that—than the stupidity and mismanagement of the unfolding enterprise, coupled with the intrusion of disease, that made the Indians extinct in so short a time.

Living in Samaná off and on over these last years has without question made me Indian-minded in reading those chronicles. I find them horrifying. Whatever consequences the first voyage of Columbus may have had for the planet and for our present existence, I cannot see that the ensuing thirty years were other than a human disaster for Hispaniola, a record of cruel and pointless conquest that could have been otherwise. Pucho asks me a lot about the Tainos—I once read him from Las Casas the descriptions of their common crops and agricultural practices, and he was as startled as I was that everything was all still growing within shouting distance, that we were more or less enacting the Tainos' agricultural patterns, using their words, living more or less as they did except for our clothes and our discontents. Even though the Tainos were his precursors rather than his ancestors, even though his language and his religion come from the Spaniards, it is with the Indians, the victims, that he identifies. When I told Pucho earlier this year that sometime in 1992 three caravels would sail into Samaná Bay, past our beach, to anchor off Las Flechas, and some actor would come ashore in a Columbus suit, he was all for gathering a few picked men from the *vecindad* and taking the actor hostage, as a gesture.

Listening to the Spanish spoken in the Dominican Republic, I quite often come on words so bizarrely unfamiliar that I have to reach their meaning by scrutinous questioning, for I have never heard them anywhere else. One such word, of Afro-Hispanic origin, from the language arrived at by the Africans brought as slaves to Hispaniola, is the noun *fucú* or *fukú*. It is often spoken with a certain dropping of the voice. *Un fucú* is something ill-omened, likely to bring bad luck, something in a person or a place or a happening that has doom about it. At the materialization of a *fucú* in any form, Dominicans cross their index fingers in the air and exclaim "*Zafa!*"—loosely translated as "Change the subject." At least they used to, I am told by the elders in my neighborhood: perhaps the custom has waned because there are so many obvious public *fucús* in the country now that the day would be one long "*Zafa!*" The word has entered not just my vocabulary but my consciousness; I am able to realize that some people and elements in New York have a *fucú* about them for me. It helps me save time.

The most interesting *fucú* of all among Dominicans, however, is the superstition that has existed for centuries that bad luck would dog anyone who spoke aloud the name of Cristóbal Colón. That called for instant crossed fingers and a loud "*Zafa!*" One referred instead to the Admiral, or the discoverer. The official propaganda surrounding the quincentenary has had to face down the *fucú*, as it were, for the name has somehow kept coming up. But the campesinos still believe in the *fucú* that C———C—— brings bad luck, perhaps with more fervor now than before. One of my neighbors told me solemnly that the word *colonia*—"colony"—came from the name of Cristóbal Colón, an error I saw no point in correcting.

It seems to me salutary that some serious arguments over Columbus and the Spanish Conquest should arise at this precise stage in our global history, since they raise disturbing questions about the meanings and evaluations of the past—questions that matter not to historians alone. We live in a postcolonial world, and we have, in our time, grown steadily more adamant about human rights, more sensitive to their violation. It seems to me that this must inevitably affect our reading and reassessment of history. It is why we now gravitate to seeing the conquest through the eyes of Las Casas rather than those of Columbus, and why we are grateful for his clarity, his humanity, and his indignation. We may argue about human rights, for they are, in a sense, abstractions, but we do not argue about human wrongs. We recognize them physically; we can point to them, in the past as in the present. Shame and indignation are our measures, as they were to Las Casas. Confronting human wrongs is our common cause at present. About the wrongs of the past we can do nothing, but we can at least look at them squarely, and see them clearly.

INTRODUCTION

The Myth of America

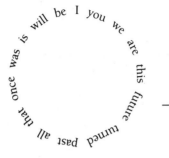

—FRANCISCO X. ALARCÓN
"Snake Wheel,"
in *Snake Poems:
An Aztec Invocation*

Of all the blessings and curses brought to this hemisphere along with Columbus five hundred years ago, none is more far-reaching than the myth of America itself. America is a European invention: until Columbus the notion never existed. We know now the globe's configuration of lands and oceans, which of course preceded our discovery of it. But before Columbus there was no America to fill our minds, only a collection of peoples scattered through a hemisphere that was not recognized as such.

Certainly our American history goes back beyond the comparatively recent fury of events unleashed by invaders and settlers from all the lands of Europe. But our history making—our self-conscious historical sense as Americans—began with Columbus, forged by the original inhabitants of the hemisphere and the new arrivals together, although seldom in cooperation.

All civilizations need a mythical dimension in order to grow and develop. Experience turns to history, and history to myth (which in turn informs experience). The subject of this book, the encounter between the Europeans and the Americans they discovered, and the forging of a new order out of that confrontation, is the root of our new American mythology.

Neither the old myths of the Americas nor those of Europe

were sufficient for the world that was produced by the cataclysmic meeting of two alien cultures. The discovery and conquest
inaugurated a long and still continuing process of reformulation
of the mythology underlying our culture.

The root of myth is language (as Claude Lévi-Strauss has
shown). Language, in the words of nineteenth-century philolo-
gist Wilhelm von Humboldt (brother of the explorer of the
Americas), draws a "magic circle" around a culture: "Man lives
with his objects chiefly—in fact, since his feeling and acting
depends on his perceptions, one may say exclusively—as language presents them to him. By the same process whereby he
spins language out of his own being, he ensnares himself in it;
and each language draws a magic circle from which there is no
escape save by stepping out of it into another."

So it is that literary artists are our foremost myth makers
today. Writers have continually sought to explore and redefine
the essence of our past, like the American poet Charles Olson,
who saw his work as an effort to reach backward "to fill a
mythological space."

Many of us have, like Alastair Reid, viewed the coming of
October 12, 1992, "with a certain dread." We have been bom-
barded with hype, hoopla, and hysteria about Columbus and
the quincentenary of his landing on our shores. But Columbus
did change the world. The early history of our hemisphere
affects us still. In this book we offer a personal panorama of the
major themes and figures of the first century or so of our post-
Columbian history: that critical time when the course of our
future was set.

The conquest of paradise—as Columbus biographer Kirkpatrick Sale has cunningly termed it—has entered the collective
imagination of our culture. It has become an essential part of
what it means to be an American, a constantly evolving shared
memory that poets and essayists and fiction writers are continually redefining. This anthology includes writings from the time
of Columbus to the present: by participants such as Columbus
himself, and explorers and conquistadores such as Amerigo

Vespucci, Hernán Cortés, and Gaspar de Carvajal; by religious figures such as Bartolomé de Las Casas, Bernardino de Sahagún, Pope Paul III, and the jaguar priests of the Maya; by historians, theorists, and essayists such as Octavio Paz, Carlos Fuentes, Tzvetan Todorov, and Malcolm Margolin; and by modern literary artists such as Abel Posse, B. Traven, Alice Walker, and Alejo Carpentier. Contemporary writers with blood ties to our pre-Columbian past include Jimmie Durham, Leslie Marmon Silko, Michael Dorris and Louise Erdrich, and Gerald Vizenor. Here will be found both native voices and those with accents of England, Spain, France, and Italy, and also writing from throughout the hemisphere: North America, Central America and the Caribbean, and South America.

As Americans, we are learning what the original Americans seem already to have known, that the land imposes itself on those who live in it, as much as the reverse. As we cultivate our ethnic heritages, we need also to recognize that we share an American heritage that has its roots in the encounter between the first Americans and the Europeans who conquered them.

As our best writers have recognized, the seeds of many current problems were planted by the same early explorers and colonists who, arriving here from an already despoiled Europe, described America as a paradise. We need not be direct descendants of the original Americans—our forebears in spirit—to feel the pain and sorrow of the devastation that raged across our hemisphere. We cannot heal that pain by denying it. We must come to terms with our early history, for we are still determining the legacy of the conquest.

Exquisite fruits of the New World. (1572)

1

PARADISE:
A Marvelous New World

Unfortunately, it was Paradise

COLUMBUS, in Abel Posse's
The Dogs of Paradise

■■

From Genesis to Genocide

Gonzalo Fernández de Oviedo, a new arrival, tries out the fruit of the New World.

The guava seems to him much superior to the apple.

The guanábana is pretty to look at and offers a white, watery pulp of very mild flavor, which, however much you eat of it, causes neither harm nor indigestion.

The mamey has a finger-licking flavor and smells very good. *Nothing better exists*, he finds.

But he bites into a medlar, and an aroma unequaled even by musk invades his head. *The medlar is the best fruit*, he corrects himself, *and nothing comparable can be found*.

Then he peels a pineapple. The golden pine smells as peaches would like to and is able to give an appetite to people who have forgotten the joys of eating. Oviedo knows no words worthy of describing its virtues. It delights his eyes, his nose, his fingers, his tongue. *This outdoes them all, as the feathers of the peacock outshine those of any bird*.

> —EDUARDO GALEANO, "For Love of Fruit
> (Santa María del Darién, 1514),"
> in *Memory of Fire: Genesis*

For European explorers America was a new Eden, and they were quick to take a bite of its tempting fruit.

The story of the first century of European involvement in this hemisphere is one of tremendous destruction, of genocide beyond any other period in history. Several million Taino Indians were killed on the island of Hispaniola alone, within twenty-five years of Columbus's first landing. Every last member of this once-thriving culture had been exterminated in less than a century. Elsewhere the story was similar. Damage to the land, which had been carefully husbanded by the Americans (whose agriculture was superior to that of the Europeans), was almost as great. The Europeans ravaged America as they settled it.

Yet for one brief period there was a profound agreement: this was paradise. Here was the best of everything: the best fruits, the best harbors and beaches, the best people in the world.

Columbus trumpeted his marvelous discovery (and possession) of an earthly paradise to anyone who would listen. Columbus's rhapsodic accounts of an earthly paradise may have started as a ploy to obtain royal support, but they eventually became a personal obsession. Columbus became convinced that he was not merely the discoverer of the New World, but the rediscoverer of the Garden of Eden.

In Spain Columbus's reports inspired contemporary historian Peter Martyr to envision the first encounter with Americans thus: "All the women were lovely. One might have supposed one were seeing those splendid naiads or those nymphs of the springs so celebrated by Antiquity. Holding up palm fronds, which they carried while performing their dances, accompanied by songs, they knelt and presented them to the governor."

Columbus was the first and perhaps the most vocal in his claim to have discovered an earthly paradise, but his contemporaries and the explorers who followed him in the seventeenth century all described America as a land of marvels, where, as Amerigo Vespucci said, "wonderful things are being discovered every day." In this sweet land, "forests [are] full of honey out of which wine is prepared and other things are made, and the farther you go into the country the more fertile you will find it," wrote Ulrich Schmidt, a Bavarian adventurer, of his travels in South America.

It *was* paradise. The geographer Carl Sauer, one of the most authoritative voices on Columbus and the early Spanish Main, wrote of the Taino culture that Columbus encountered: "The economy worked because production of the land was in balance with food taken from the water, and the bounty of the waters also was great." Consequently, observes Sauer (in *The Early Spanish Main*), "The tropical idyll of the accounts of Columbus and Peter Martyr was largely true. The people suffered no want. They took care of their plantings, were dextrous at fishing and bold canoeists and swimmers. They designed attractive houses and kept them clean. They found aesthetic expression in woodworking. They had leisure to enjoy diversion in ballgames, dances, and music. They lived in peace and amity."

Very quickly, however, the Europeans learned to view this paradise in their own image, to find the evil lurking within, a web of evil spun by Satan, a devil who held up his glass to reveal debasement and dark motives. "In confronting the more puzzling features of alien societies," scholar J. H. Elliott wrote in "The Discovery of America and the Discovery of Man," "a sixteenth-century Europe obsessed with the cosmic conflict between God and the devil found the answers to its puzzlement in the *diabolus ex machina*."

Still, it was the European arrivals who did the greater share of the devil's work in the end.

Christopher Columbus

The Breast of Paradise

Not the first to discover this hemisphere, not even the first to cross the Atlantic to reach it, Columbus remains in many respects first in the lore of the Americas. He was the first to announce the discovery of paradise, just as he was the first to torture, murder, and enslave the people who lived in it. Only the voice of Columbus could lead the chorus of voices in this book with the fantastic poetry, the "magical realism," of his assertion that he had located Eden in the form of a nipple on the breast of the world.

As schoolchildren we may have been told that in medieval times the world was thought to be flat, and that Columbus overturned this view by arguing that the world was round. In fact, as this passage shows, Columbus insisted, against the prevailing wisdom, that the world was not round.

Columbus's argument here relies in part on his navigational observations. But how good a sailor was he? Some scholars praise, others question his navigational abilities. Columbus's voyage of discovery had been his first command, won at court through his political skills and powers of persuasion over the queen rather than by merit on the sea. While the experienced captains of the PINTA *and* NIÑA *had no difficulty navigating the easy, uneventful crossing of the first voyage, Columbus, in charge of the* SANTA MARÍA, *ran aground in harbor on a clear and windless night. (Columbus concluded that God had chosen this means of communicating to him a good place to stop and build a fort.)*

It was not his sailing ability that had led Columbus to Eden. He felt it was a divine mandate. Didn't his very name make his heroic role obvious? Christopher, "bearer of Christ." In America Columbus's thoughts grew more and more tortured. In the course of his brief but difficult third voyage (he held command only three weeks), in which he reached the mainland of South America, Columbus became delusional. On 18 October 1498, he reported his discovery of paradise to Ferdinand and Isabella, in a letter Kirkpatrick Sale characterizes as "a very long and muddled mishmash of theology and astronomy and geography and fantastic lore, rambling, repetitive, illogical, confusing, at times incoherent, self-serving, servile and vainglorious all at once—and quite loony."

Allegations that Columbus was a miserable governor, a poor leader, an opportunist, and an unfit navigator were gathering support. In Hispaniola, where Columbus had established the first colony of Europeans in America, a group of Spaniards under the lead of Francisco Roldán revolted. According to Columbus biographer Gianni Granzotto, Roldán was inspired by his own notion of paradise: he was "attracted to the beauty of the land and the gentleness of the Indians' customs."

Columbus's voyage was cut short by royal command. Not long after his announcement of the discovery of the earthly paradise, Columbus was returned to Spain in chains.

In his influential biography of his father, Fernando Columbus neglected to mention the discovery of Eden.

The heat became so great, the rays of the sun so intense, that I thought I would go up in smoke. Even when rains came and the sky was overcast, still my strength was sapped, until Our Lord sent a provident breeze that led me to head west, for I thought that somehow, once I reached the line of the equinox, the heat would abate. And indeed when I reached it the weather turned mild, and as I went forward it grew even milder, though I could not account for this by plotting my course by the stars. When

night came on the polestar was five degrees high, at midnight it
was at ten degrees, and by daybreak at fifteen. The sea remained
smooth but the vegetation had greatly changed. I was mystified
by the polestar's odd behavior, and I spent many nights studying
it with the quadrant, and always the results were the same. This
was a new discovery, indicating that in this small space the sky
changes dramatically.

Everything I have read says that the world, both land and
water, is spherical; the authoritative accounts and the experiments of Ptolemy and all the others have verified and confirmed
this by study of the eclipses of the moon and other east-west phe-
nomena, as well as of the elevation of the pole star from north to
south. But, as I have just said, I had now discovered a great ir-
regularity in my own observations, so that I have made the following conclusion: the world is not round as they describe it. It
is shaped like a pear that is round except for the protuberance
where the stem is, where it swells up. It's like a round ball that
has something like a woman's nipple on one part of it, and there,
where that protuberance is found, it rises high into the sky, precisely at the line of the equinox in the Ocean Sea at the end of
the East, the end of the east where there is no more land, no more
islands. . . .

Where I began my voyage, the people are very black and the
land is scorched by the sun; then I passed through Cape Verde,
where the people are even blacker, and the more I continued
southward, the blacker they became. . . . But after I passed the
line of which I have spoken, I found that the temperature grew
milder until, when I reached the island of Trinidad, where the
North Star rose five degrees when night began, and also in the
land I call Gracia, I found quite a mild climate where the land
and the trees are as green and lovely as the orchard of Valencia
in April. And the people are very fair, whiter than the others I
have seen in the Indies, and their hair is long and smooth, and
they are shrewder and more intelligent, and they are not cow-
ards. The sun was in Virgo, over our heads and theirs. And this

must be because of the mild climate, which in turn is because of this land being the highest in the world, nearest to the sky, as I have said. And so I repeat, the world is not round. . . .

Holy scripture testifies that Our Lord made the earthly paradise and in it placed the tree of life, and from it issues a fountain that produces the four great rivers of the world, the Ganges, the Tigris, the Euphrates, and the Nile. I do not find in any of the writings of the Romans or Greeks anything that establishes the location of this earthly paradise, nor have I seen it authoritatively placed on any map of the world. I do not believe that the earthly paradise is in the form of a rugged mountain as it has been described. Instead, I believe that it is at the summit of this pearlike protuberance, to which one can gradually ascend. . . . I believe that the fresh water I have discovered on this journey originates there. . . .

Here I have found all the signs of this earthly paradise.

Christopher Columbus

New World Rhapsodies

Although stopping short of claiming to have discovered paradise, Co-
lumbus was greatly pleased with himself and with the world through-
out his first encounter with America, as this garland of lyrical excerpts
from the log of his first voyage shows. He was as enchanted by the
Americans (although disappointed by their nakedness, which did not
suggest riches) as by the land they inhabited.

Yet "the ecology Columbus described was never really there," Co-
lumbus biographer Felipe Fernández-Armesto has noted. "This was
promotional writing. But it was also poetry."

Columbus's expansive mood did not last. Little more than a decade
later, on 7 July 1503, shipwrecked on Jamaica and his world collapsing
upon him, he wrote his royal patrons that he was "surrounded by a mil-
lion savages filled with cruelty and inimical to us."

This land is all so lush and its weather such a delight that I love
to look out upon it. In fact, since we left the Canaries, God has
not failed to provide one perfect day after the other. And the
people are so gentle! (13 *October* 1492) There are groves of the
most beautiful trees I have ever seen. They are as green and
leafy as those of Spain in April and May, and there are many
ponds and lakes. (14 *October*) The trees I walked among today are

the most beautiful I have ever seen. . . . This is a very green, level, and fertile island, and I have no doubt that the people sow and reap grain, and also many other things, year round. I saw many trees quite different from ours. Many of them have branches of different kinds, all on the same trunk; one twig is of one kind and another of another, and so different from each other that it is the greatest wonder in the world. . . . On one tree there will grow five or six different kinds of plants, all of them different. (17 *October*) This island is the most beautiful I have ever seen; the others are beautiful, but this is even more so. (19 *October*) The other islands are very green and beautiful and fertile, but this one is much more so, with great and green groves of trees. There are some large lagoons and above and around them is the most wonderful wooded area. (21 *October*) I have never seen anything so beautiful. The country around the river is full of trees, beautiful and green and different from ours, each with flowers and its own kind of fruit. (28 *October*) The houses of these Indians are the most beautiful I have ever seen, and I swear that the closer I get to the mainland, the better they become. They're like grand pavilions, like royal tents in an encampment without streets. One here, another there. They are well swept and quite clean inside, and the furnishings are arranged in good order. All are built of very beautiful palm branches. . . . The island is so beautiful, I could go on praising it forever. And there are trees with wonderful-tasting fruit. . . . The song of the crickets in the night are an enchantment, and the evening air is sweet and fragrant. And the mountains are beautiful and high. (29 *October*) The entire country is low and beautiful, and the sea is very deep. (30 *October*) This is one of the best harbors in the world; this is the best climate; these are the friendliest people. (5 *November*) There are no higher mountains anywhere in the world than those I have seen these past few days. They are the most beautiful and clear, without fog or snow, and at the base the sea is very deep. . . . Some of the mountains appear to climb to Heaven itself; they are like the points of diamonds. (14 *November*) This entire country consists of very high and beautiful mountains that are not dry or rocky but entirely accessible; there are also the most delightful valleys. The valleys as well as the mountains are covered with tall and verdant trees, which are a delight to behold. (26 *November*) It was so marvelous to see the forests and greenery, the crystal clear water, the birds, and the ideal location, that I could hardly bear to leave this place. The loveliness of this country surpasses all others, as daylight exceeds night. (27 *November*) All the trees are green and full of fruit, and the plants are in flower and quite tall. The roads are wide and good, and the breezes are like those of Castile in the month of April. The nightingales and other small birds sing as they do in Spain in the same month, and this is the greatest pleasure in all the world. (13 *December*) This country is the best that language can describe. . . . In all Castile no land can be compared to this in beauty and fertility. (16 *December*) This harbor surpasses any that I have ever seen. I have said such fine things about previous ones that it is difficult to find the words to describe this one. Yet my fine descriptions of earlier harbors were true—still this is better than all the rest. . . . Indeed, this is truly the finest harbor in the whole world, and all the ships in the world could lie together in it. (21 *December*) There cannot be better or more gentle people than these anywhere in the world. . . . Their houses and settlements are very attractive, governed by a chief or judge whom all obey. These chiefs are men of few words and fine manners, and it is a marvel. (24 *December*)

Amerigo Vespucci

Mundus Novus

Amerigo Vespucci, a representative of Italian commercial interests in Spain, was part of an expedition to South America in 1499. Columbus, who was anxious to discover the mainland, had already reached South America in 1498, but he had turned away from it. Vespucci, piecing together his own experience with the reports of Columbus's voyage, concluded that a new continent had in fact been discovered.

Vespucci not only gave his name to the hemisphere, but also popularized the phrase "the New World." His pamphlet MUNDUS NOVUS *("New World") was a best-seller in the early sixteenth century (it was probably not by Vespucci but rather was ghost authored or pirated from his papers and documents). With Columbus there was a doubt: Had he discovered a new world? Was he retracing the paths of sailors of antiquity? Had he reached the Indies as he sometimes claimed? But Vespucci or his ghost author voiced no uncertainty: they heralded the discovery of a new world, a world "prolix and vast."*

First then as to the people. We found in those parts such a multitude of people as nobody could enumerate (as we read in the Apocalypse), a race I say gentle and amenable. All of both sexes go about naked, covering no part of their bodies; and just as they spring from their mothers' wombs so they go until death. They have indeed large square-built bodies, well formed and proportioned, and in color verging upon reddish. This I think has come to them, because, going about naked, they are colored by the sun. They have, too, hair plentiful and black. In their gait and when playing their games they are agile and dignified. They are comely, too, of countenance which they nevertheless themselves destroy; for they bore their cheeks, lips, noses and ears. Nor think those holes small or that they have one only. For some I have seen having in a single face seven borings any one of which was capable of holding a plum. They stop up these holes of theirs with blue stones, bits of marble, very beautiful crystals of alabaster, very white bones, and other things artificially prepared according to their customs. But if you could see a thing so unwonted and monstrous, that is to say a man having in his cheeks and lips alone seven stones, some of which are a span and a half in length, you would not be without wonder. For I frequently observed and discovered that seven such stones weighed sixteen ounces aside from the fact that in their ears, each perforated with three holes, they have other stones dangling on rings; and this usage applies to the men alone. For women do not bore their faces, but their ears only. They have another custom, very shameful and beyond all human belief. For their women, being very lustful, cause the private parts of their husbands to swell up to such a huge size that they appear deformed and disgusting; and this is accomplished by a certain device of theirs, the biting of certain poisonous animals. And in consequence of this many lose their organs which break through lack of attention, and they remain eunuchs. They have no cloth either of wool, linen or cotton, since they need it not; neither do they have goods of their own, but all things are held in common. They live together without king, without government, and each is his own master. They marry as many wives as they please; and son cohabits with mother, brother with sister, male cousin with female, and any man with the first woman he meets. They dissolve their marriages as often as they please, and observe no sort of law with respect to them. Beyond the fact that they have no church, no religion and are not idolaters, what more can I say? They live according to nature, and may be called Epicureans rather than Stoics. There are no merchants among their number, nor is there barter. The nations wage war upon one another without art or order. The elders by means of certain harangues of theirs bend the youths to their will and inflame them to wars in which they cruelly kill one another, and those whom they bring home captives from war they preserve, not to spare their lives, but that they may be slain for food; for they eat one another, the victors the vanquished, and among other kinds of meat human flesh is a common article of diet with them. Nay be the more assured of this fact because the father has already been seen to eat children and wife, and I knew a man whom I also spoke to who was reputed to have eaten more than three hundred human bodies. And I likewise remained twenty-seven days in a certain city where I saw salted human flesh suspended from beams between the houses, just as with us it is the custom to hang pork. I say further: they themselves wonder why we do not eat our enemies and do not use as food their flesh which they say is most savory. Their weapons are bows and arrows, and when they advance to war they cover no part of their bodies for the sake of protection, so like beasts are they in this matter. We endeavored to the extent of our power to dissuade them and persuade them to desist from these depraved customs, and they did promise us that they would leave off. The women as I have said go about naked and are very libidinous; yet they have bodies which are tolerably beautiful and cleanly. Nor are they so unsightly as one perchance might imagine; for, inasmuch as they are plump, their ugliness is the less apparent, which indeed is for the most part concealed by the excellence of their bodily structure. It was to us a matter of astonishment that none was to be seen among them who had a flabby breast, and those who had borne children were not to be distinguished from virgins by the shape of and shrinking of the womb; and in the other parts of the body similar things were seen of which in the interest of modesty I make no mention. When they had the opportunity of copulating with Christians, urged by excessive lust, they defiled and prostituted themselves.

They live one hundred and fifty years, and rarely fall ill, and if they do fall victims to any disease, they cure themselves with certain roots and herbs. These are the most noteworthy things I know about them. The climate there was very temperate and good, and as I was able to learn from their accounts, there was never there any pest or epidemic caused by corruption of the air; and unless they die a violent death they live long. This I take to be because the south winds are ever blowing there, and especially that which we call Eurus, which is the same to them as the Aquilo is to us. They are zealous in the art of fishing, and that sea is replete and abounding in every kind of fish. They are not hunters. This I deem to be because there are there many sorts of wild animals, and especially lions and bears and innumerable serpents and other horrid and ugly beasts, and also because forests and trees of huge size there extend far and wide; and they dare not, naked and without covering and arms, expose themselves to such hazards. The land in those parts is very fertile and pleasing, abounding in numerous hills and mountains, boundless valleys and mighty rivers, watered by refreshing springs, and filled with broad, dense and well nigh impenetrable forests full of every sort of wild animal. Trees grow to immense size without cultivation. Many of these yield fruits delectable to the taste and beneficial to the human body; some indeed do not, and no fruits there are like those of ours. Innumerable species of herbs and roots grow there too, of which they make bread and excellent food. They have, too, many seeds altogether unlike these of ours. They have there no metals of any description except gold, of which those regions have a great plenty, although to be sure we have brought none thence on this our first voyage. This the natives called to our attention, who averred that in the districts remote from the coast there is a great abundance of gold, and by them it is in no respect esteemed or valued. They are rich in pearls as I wrote you before. If I were to seek to recount in detail what things are there and to write concerning the numerous species of animals and the great number of them, it would be a matter all too prolix and vast. And I truly believe that our Pliny did not touch upon a thousandth part of the species of parrots and other birds and the animals, too, which exist in those same regions so diverse as to form and color; because Policletus, the master of painting in all its perfection, would have fallen short in depicting them. There all trees are fragrant and they emit each and all gum, oil, or some sort of sap. If the properties of these were known to us, I doubt not but that they would be salutary to the human body. And surely if the terrestrial paradise be in any part of this earth, I esteem that it is not far distant from those parts.

Evan S. Connell, Jr.

Paradise Abandoned

Several hundred years before Columbus's landfall, Norsemen voyaged to America, fished its coastal waters, and settled its lands. Columbus may have heard the sagas that tell of their voyages, perhaps in a visit to Galway, Ireland. As Evan Connell reports in THE WHITE LANTERN, *in a chapter entitled "Vinland Vínland," existing copies from as early as the fourteenth century of "The Greenlanders' Saga" and two versions of "Eirik's saga" tell the story of Leif Eriksson and his fearsome half sister Freydis.*

The sagas report several expeditions to America. The first was that of an Icelander, Bjarni Herjolfsson, who was blown off course in a voyage to Greenland. Leif bought Bjarni's boat and retraced his journey. The opening selection from "Vinland Vínland" describes the attractive lands that Leif encountered in the company of his German godfather, Tyrkir, whose discovery of grapes caused his godson to name the new region Vinland.

Two of Leif's brothers, Thorsvald and Thorstein, also made trips to Vinland. Both died, but Thorstein's wife Gudrid remarried, and with her new husband, Thorfinn Karlsefni, she led one of the most significant of the Norse expeditions. The failure of this colonization attempt, which included sixty men, five women, and livestock, is described in the second selection from "Vinland Vínland."

When Gudrid's party, landed in America, discovered a group of sleeping Indians, (whom they called skraelings) they killed them at once. Relations with the natives became strained, and many battles were waged. Leif's half sister Freydis is the most dramatic figure in the story of this expedition. Once, when the Norsemen were in full retreat, Freydis pulled her breasts out of her garment, raised a sword she had drawn from a fallen Viking, and whetted it across her chest. Freydis was a formidable woman. Her gesture threw her attackers into a panic: "They were aghast and fled to the boats. . . . "

Gudrid gave birth to a son in America before returning to Iceland. (She is said later to have traveled to Rome and become a nun.) The terrible Freydis led the next expedition, a joint venture between her own Greenlanders and an Icelandic group. Once disembarked in America, Freydis set about getting the Icelanders killed. After the Greenlanders had killed the men from Iceland, Freydis personally slew all five of the Icelandic women with an ax.

When Leif Eriksson learned of Freydis's deeds, he prophesied that "no good will come to you and your descendants." In this first recorded European attempt to colonize America, as in the later dramas enacted by Columbus and the other European invaders, paradise quickly turned to perdition.

They came to the forest land, which they named Markland. It sounds agreeable, "with white sandy beaches shelving gently toward the sea," yet according to the sagas Leif and his men stayed only a short time before hurrying back to their ship as fast as they could. The sagas do not explain why they were anxious to leave. Nor do we know exactly where they were, though it must have been either Labrador or Nova Scotia.

Two days later they reached an island and went ashore. The weather was fine. They saw dew on the grass, which they tasted, "and they thought that never had they tasted anything as sweet." After this they returned to the ship and entered the sound which lay between the island and a cape projecting northward from the mainland.

They sailed westward past this cape. The water was very

shallow. At low tide the ship touched bottom, "and it was a long way from the ship to the sea. But they were so impatient to get to land that they did not want to wait for the tide to rise under their ship but ran ashore at a place where a river flowed out of a lake."

As soon as the tide refloated the ship they brought it up into the lake. Here they anchored, unloaded some sacks of hide, and built stone-and-turf huts. Later, after deciding to winter at this place, they built houses. The lake and river were full of huge salmon and they thought cattle would be able to survive without fodder. There was no frost and the grass scarcely withered.

When the house-building had been completed Leif divided his men. Each day one group went out to explore the countryside, with orders that they should not become separated and that they return by dusk. At first things went well, but one evening Tyrkir was missing. Leif was very much disturbed because Tyrkir had been one of his father's companions for a long time.

"Leif spoke harsh words. . . ."

Twelve men set out to find Tyrkir. They had not gone far when he showed up. He was obviously in a good mood, rolling his eyes and laughing and talking in German so that nobody understood what he was saying. "The Greenlanders' Saga" describes him as being small, dark, and seedy in appearance, with a sloping forehead and an unsteady eye, but good at all kinds of odd jobs.

"Why are you so late, foster-father?" asked Leif. "And why did you leave your comrades?"

Tyrkir continued laughing, grimacing, and talking in German. Finally he spoke in Norse. "I have some news for you," he said. "I have found vines with grapes."

"Is that true, foster-father?" Leif asked.

"Of course it's true." said Tyrkir, "because where I was born there are plenty of vines and grapes."

Next morning Leif instructed his men to pick grapes and cut vines and to begin felling trees so that when they returned to Greenland they would have a good cargo. And when they embarked in the spring their ship carried a load of grapes, vines, and timber. Leif named the place Vinland.

*   *   *

Not much is left. There is the ground plan of a big turf-walled house—fifty by seventy feet, with five or six rooms—and the outlines of various smaller structures including a smithy, a bath-house, five boat sheds, a kiln, and two cooking pits.

Very little handiwork has survived, partly because there is so much acid in the soil. Almost everything made of bone or wood has disintegrated, whatever was not carried off by Eskimos, Indians, and early Newfoundland settlers. There are rusty traces that once were nails, a piece of copper with cross stripings that might have come from a belt, a whetstone, a bone needle, a bit of jasper, a stone lamp of the old Icelandic type, a steatite spindle whorl—meaning there were women in the house —and a bronze ring-headed pin. Pins of this type were used by Vikings to fasten their capes. And in the smithy was a large cracked flat-topped stone—the anvil—together with scraps of bog iron, clumps of slag, and patches of soot.

The great house burned, says Dr. Helge Ingstad, who supervised the excavation, although it is impossible to say whether this happened by accident or design.

L'Anse aux Meadows must have been an agreeable place to live. There were fields of berries and flowers, salmon in the lake, herds of caribou—many more animals and birds than there are now. The sea was alive with cod, seals, and whales, and the weather probably was mild.

Then why was Paradise abandoned? And why is there no sign of other settlements?

The answer seems to be that these people arrived too soon. Europe was not ready to support them, and with only spears, axes, knives, and swords these few colonists could not hold out against the skraelings. Whether they were killed in one overwhelming raid, whether they intermarried with the natives, or perhaps moved farther south, or at last gave up and retreated to Greenland—neither the ruins nor the old vellum manuscripts reveal.

Ralph Lane

Goodliest Roanoke

Colonization of North America lagged behind that of the territories claimed by the Spanish and Portuguese, but it followed a similar pattern. The first attempt to establish an English colony was made on Roanoke Island nearly a century after Columbus's initial voyage. In command was Ralph Lane, who, in the following brief excerpt from a September 1685 letter to Richard Hakluyt, adds his voice to the general exultation about the discovery of a rich new land.

Lane, a military man, was ill equipped to manage the colony. Despite his inventory of agricultural goods in this passage, the English colonists produced nothing on their own at Roanoke; they lived on corn and fish stolen from nearby Americans. Periodically they launched raiding attacks, but they failed to conquer their American neighbors, who often got the better of them in these skirmishes.

Roanoke may have been a paradise, but when Sir Francis Drake happened by and offered passage to England, not a single settler chose to stay.

We have discovered the main to be the goodliest soil under the cope of heaven, so abounding with sweet trees, that bring such sundry and most pleasant gums, grapes of such greatness, yet wild, as France, Spain nor Italy hath no greater, so many sorts of

Apothecary drugs, such several kinds of flax, and one kind of silk, the same gathered of a grass as common there as grass is here. And now within these few days we have found here a Guinea wheat, whose ear yieldeth corn for bread, 400 upon one ear, and the cane maketh very good and perfect sugar. . . .

[This land] is very well peopled and towned, though savagely, and the climate so wholesome that we have not had one sick since we touched land here. To conclude, if Virginia had but horses and kine in some reasonable proportion, I dare assure myself, being inhabited with English, no realm of Christendom were comparable to it.

Henri Joutel

Abundance in the Gulf Coast

The paradise of Henri Joutel is far from the tortured religious construction of Columbus. In this excerpt from a nineteenth-century translation of his 1685 JOURNAL HISTORIQUE, Joutel appears to be a man enjoying life and the beauty of the world around him—which is all the more admirable, since his circumstances at the time were difficult indeed.

Joutel is a much keener observer of nature than Columbus. He is as appreciative of "a sort of purple wind flower" as he is of the "many sorts of fowl fit to eat." His account of the abundance of life in the Gulf Coast reveals the sharp eye of a practical man who would be unlikely to be forced to steal corn and fish from the natives to survive, as did the Englishman Lane.

Joutel was among René-Robert La Salle's party of French explorers. In 1673 the French team of Marquette and Joliet had traveled a good way down the Mississippi and were fairly certain it flowed into the Gulf of Mexico. Armed with this geographical insight, La Salle conceived the plan for a grand French trade network extending from the St. Lawrence to the Gulf of Mississippi.

The first step was to sail down the river as far as its mouth, which the La Salle party did. Next they had to approach the river mouth by sea. Joutel was a volunteer on this voyage—and one of its few survivors. On a foggy New Year's Day in 1685, La Salle and Joutel were separated from their captain and most of their fleet. They tried to locate the mouth of the Mississippi, but La Salle's navigation was not sophisticated; he was not a sailor. Finally they reached the Bay of Matagorda, about four hundred miles west of the Mississippi, near present-day Houston, Texas.

Deciding this was the Mississippi, the Frenchmen threw up a rickety fort. They were not deluded for long. Leaving Joutel in charge, La Salle began a series of voyages in search of the Mississippi. After two years, he had still not found it. And he had lost 135 of his original 180 colonists. Joutel remained loyal, but unfortunately for La Salle others did not. He was murdered in January 1687, without ever having found the mighty Mississippi.

Life cannot have been easy for Joutel in Matagorda. Yet he could exult in the beauty and abundance of this new paradise—another paradise that ended in disaster and defeat.

We were near the bay of St. Louis and the bank of the River aux Boeufs, on a little hillock, whence we discovered vast and beautiful plains, extending very far to the westward, all level and full of greens, which afford pasture to an infinite number of beeves and other creatures.

Between a little hill and our dwelling was a sort of marsh, and in it abundance of wild fowl, as curlews, water hens and other sorts. In the marsh there were also little pools full of fish. We also had an infinite number of beeves, wild goats, rabbits, turkeys, bustards, geese, swans, fieldfares, plovers, teal, partridges and many other sorts of fowl fit to eat, and among them one called le grand gosier, or the great gullet, because it has a very large one; another as big and fleshy as a pullet, which we called the spatula, because its beak is shaped like one, and the feather of it being a pale red, are very beautiful. The river supplied us with abundance of other fishes, whose names we knew not. The gulf afforded us oysters, eels, trout, a sort of red fishes and others, whose long, sharp and hard beak tore all our nets. We had plenty both of land and sea tortoises, whose eggs served to season our sauces. The land tortoises differ from those of the sea, as being smaller, round, and their shell more beautiful. They hide themselves in holes they find or make in the earth.

There are abundance of creeping vines, and others that run up the bodies and to the tops of trees, which bear plenty of grapes, fleshy and sharp, not to compare to the delicacy of ours in Europe; but we made verjuice of them, which was very good in sauce. Mulberry trees are numerous along the rivers.

Nothing is more beautiful than to behold those vast plains when the blossoms appear. I have observed some that smelt like a tuberose, but the leaf resembles our borage. I have seen primroses having a scent like ours, African gilliflowers, and a sort of purple wind flower.

Fray Marcos de Niza

Marvelous Lands

The New World was indeed filled with astonishing things. And always the mysteries of revelation—and lands rich in gold—seemed to lie just beyond the horizon. The early explorers and conquerors performed incredible feats in their determination to reach these alluring lands.

From New Spain—as Mexico was known after Cortés's victory—the Spaniards sought to expand, to enjoy more of the spoils of the new land that lay before them like a ripe fruit waiting to be picked. With the startling arrival in Mexico of Cabeza de Vaca, a Spaniard who had been stranded in Galveston Bay in Florida in 1528, attention turned to the lands to the north, the lands from which the Aztecs themselves had originally come. Cabeza de Vaca had spent eight years making a land journey across the continent to Mexico, living with native Americans and learning their languages (throughout his travels he had been received courteously and assisted generously by the native peoples). His lengthy sojourn suggested the expanse of the interior of the continent of North America.

In 1539 Fray Marcos de Niza, a companion of Pedro de Alvarado, the ruthless lieutenant of Cortés and conqueror of Central America, was commissioned to explore the regions to the north. After a rather desultory exploration, the friar returned with an astonishing report of the discovery of Cíbola, one of the Seven Cities of medieval legend.

This excerpt is from a letter by Rodrigo de Albornoz, the treasurer of New Spain, describing the friar's report. Carl Sauer calls his relation "a strange tissue of hearsay, fantasy, fact, and fraud." But on the strength of his report, Francisco Vásquez de Coronado and others invested their fortunes and spent two years exploring the Colorado plateau in search of the legendary city. They "discovered" the Grand Canyon, and ultimately explored as far north as Kansas.

It was one of the longest and most arduous explorations ever accomplished in the Americas. López de Gómara described how the explorers marked their path with piles of buffalo dung as they struggled across desert and plains. Nowhere did they encounter the bounty the New World had seemed to promise. They returned destitute and defeated, and the Southwest was left relatively unspoiled for almost three hundred years thereafter.

Marvel was beginning to give way to grim reality.

There are seven very populous cities with great buildings. Of one of these the friar brought news by sight, of those farther off by hearsay. The name of the one where he has been is Cíbola, the others are in the kingdom of Marata. There is very good news of other very populous country, both of their riches and good order and the manner of their living, also of their edifices and other matters. They have houses built of stone and lime, being of three stories, and with great quantity of turquoise set in doors and windows. Of animals there are camels and elephants and cattle of our kind as well as wild ones, hunted by the natives, and a great number of sheep like those of Peru, also other animals with a single horn reaching to their feet, for which reason they must feed sideways. They say that these are not unicorns but of another kind. The people are said to go clothed to the neck in long vestments of camlet, girdled in the manner of Moors. In sum, they are known to be people of good understanding.

Gaspar de Carvajal

The River of the Amazons

In 1542, Francisco de Orellana led the first voyage down the length of the Amazon, a journey that lasted nine months. The explorers suffered numerous hardships, including many attacks from river dwellers equipped with poison darts. Among the Spanish party was a Dominican friar, Fray Gaspar de Carvajal, who left a lengthy account of the journey, THE DISCOVERY OF THE RIVER OF THE AMAZONS.

The specter of the legendary women warriors who lent their name to the river hangs over Carvajal's narrative, as in this passage in which the Spaniards believe they have discovered signs of a great civilization in a humble river settlement.

Here the New World marvels have turned to menace; they seem to presage disaster.

The nightmare came to pass in the next voyage down the river, an adventure that was celebrated in Werner Herzog's 1972 film, AGUIRRE, THE WRATH OF GOD. *That journey ended in madness and blood.*

We landed at a medium-sized village, went ashore, and mingled with the inhabitants. There was an immense public square in the village, and in its center was a hewn tree trunk ten feet in diameter. On this trunk was a carved relief showing a walled city, with the enclosure and gate. Beside the gate were two high towers, each breached by windows, each with a door that faced the other. These doors were flanked by two columns. The entire structure was resting between the forepaws and claws of two very fierce lions, which were twisting around and staring suspiciously at each other; at the center of the structure was a round open space: in the middle of this space was a hole through which the natives pour *chicha*, their wine, as an offering in honor of the Sun, for they worship the Sun and consider it their god. In short, the structure was an incredible sight, and the captain and all of us marveled at it. We seized an Indian and asked him what it was, or what meaning it held for them. The Indian answered that they were subjects of the Amazons, to whom they paid tribute, supplying them with parrot and macaw feathers, which the Amazons used to line the roofs of their temples, and that all their villages did the same, and they kept the structure as a symbol, and worshipped it as emblem of their mistress, the one who rules over all the lands controlled by those women. . . .

Malcolm Margolin

About the Bay

Throughout the Americas, anthropologists and ecologists find that for the most part peoples and lands existed in a remarkably stable and enduring balance. Native Americans were far from passive residents on the land (as many of the European Americans assumed), but actively tended and husbanded the environment.

The nature and consequences of the encounter between these Americans and the new European arrivals were everywhere about the same. While the islands of the Caribbean experienced the transformation to a post-Columbian society with astonishing rapidity, elsewhere the same dramas were played out years, decades, or, in the case of northern California, even centuries later.

Because northern California was one of the last areas of America to be explored and settled by Europeans, its "pre-Columbian" past should be nearer at hand than in most of the country. Little of that tantalizing past remains accessible, however, although only two hundred years ago—a few generations—this region was much as it had been for millennia. This passage from THE OHLONE WAY *by Malcolm Margolin illustrates the marvelous balance maintained by native Americans. The accounts on which this 1978 work is based are from as late as the nineteenth century, but the land and the relation of the inhabitants to it seem little changed from anthropological reconstructions of much earlier periods. Contrast that stability to the transformations experienced on the Eastern seaboard in the years between Columbus and the industrial society of the nineteenth century.*

Margolin describes the San Francisco Bay Area as it used to be, giving us one of the most vivid descriptions of how land, flora and fauna, and even climate were altered by the collision of two worlds, and paradise lost.

Modern residents would hardly recognize the Bay Area as it was in the days of the Ohlones. Tall, sometimes shoulder-high stands of native bunchgrasses (now almost entirely replaced by the shorter European annuals) covered the vast meadowlands and the tree-dotted savannahs. Marshes that spread out for thousands of acres fringed the shores of the Bay. Thick oak-bay forests and redwood forests covered much of the hills.

The intermingling of grasslands, savannahs, salt- and fresh-water marshes, and forests created wildlife habitats of almost unimaginable richness and variety. The early explorers and adventurers, no matter how well-travelled in other parts of the globe, were invariably struck by the plentiful animal life here. "There is not any country in the world which more abounds in fish and game of every description," noted the French sea captain La Pérouse. Flocks of geese, ducks, and seabirds were so enormous that when alarmed by a rifle shot they were said to rise "in a dense cloud with a noise like that of a hurricane." Herds of elk—"monsters with tremendous horns," as one of the early missionaries described them—grazed the meadowlands in such numbers that they were often compared with great herds of cattle. Pronghorn antelopes, in herds of one or two hundred, or even more, dotted the grassy slopes.

Packs of wolves hunted the elk, antelope, deer, rabbits, and other game. Bald eagles and giant condors glided through the air. Mountain lions, bobcats, and coyotes—now seen only rarely— were a common sight. And of course there was the grizzly bear. "He was horrible, fierce, large, and fat," wrote Father Pedro Font, an early missionary, and a most apt description it was.

These enormous bears were everywhere, feeding on berries, lumbering along the beaches, congregating beneath oak trees during the acorn season, and stationed along nearly every stream and creek during the annual runs of salmon and steelhead.

It is impossible to estimate how many thousands of bears might have lived in the Bay Area at the time of the Ohlones. Early Spanish settlers captured them readily for their famous bear-and-bull fights, ranchers shot them by the dozen to protect their herds of cattle and sheep, and the early Californians chose the grizzly as the emblem of their flag and their statehood. The histories of many California townships tell how bears collected in troops around the slaughterhouses and sometimes wandered out onto the main streets of towns to terrorize the inhabitants. To the Ohlones the grizzly bear must have been omnipresent, yet today there is not a single wild grizzly bear left in all of California.

Life in the ocean and in the unspoiled bays of San Francisco and Monterey was likewise plentiful beyond modern conception. There were mussels, clams, oysters, abalones, seabirds, and sea otters in profusion. Sea lions blackened the rocks at the entrance to San Francisco Bay and in Monterey Bay they were so abundant that to one missionary they seemed to cover the entire surface of the water "like a pavement."

Long, wavering lines of pelicans threaded the air. Clouds of gulls, cormorants, and other shore birds rose, wheeled, and screeched at the approach of a human. Rocky islands like Alcatraz (which means *pelican* in Spanish) were white from the droppings of great colonies of birds.

In the days before the nineteenth-century whaling fleets, whales were commonly sighted within the bays and along the ocean coast. An early visitor to Monterey Bay wrote: "It is impossible to conceive of the number of whales with which we were surrounded, or their familiarity; they every half minute spouted within half a pistol shot of the ships and made a prodigious stench in the air." Along the bays and ocean beaches whales were often seen washed up on shore, with grizzly bears in "countless troops"—or in many cases Indians—streaming down the beach to feast on their remains.

Nowadays, especially during the summer months, we consider most of the Bay Area to be a semi-arid country. But from the diaries of the early explorers the picture we get is of a moist, even swampy land. In the days of the Ohlones the water table was much closer to the surface, and indeed the first settlers who dug wells here regularly struck clear, fresh water within a few feet.

Water was virtually everywhere, especially where the land was flat. The explorers suffered far more from mosquitoes, spongy earth, and hard to ford rivers than they did from thirst—even in the heat of summer. Places that are now dry were then described as having springs, brooks, ponds—even fairly large lakes. In the days before channelizations, all the major rivers—the Carmel, Salinas, Pajaro, Coyote Creek, and Alameda Creek—as well as many minor streams, spread out each winter and spring to form wide, marshy valleys.

The San Francisco Bay, in the days before landfill, was much larger than it is today. Rivers and streams emptying into it often fanned out into estuaries which supported extensive tule marshes. The low, salty margins of the Bay held vast pickleweed and cordgrass swamps. Cordgrass provided what many biologists now consider to be the richest wildlife habitat in all North America.

Today only Suisun Marsh and a few other smaller areas give a hint of the extraordinary bird and animal life that the fresh- and saltwater swamps of the Bay Area once supported. Ducks were so thick that an early European hunter told how "several were frequently killed with one shot." Channels crisscrossed the Bayshore swamps—channels so labyrinthian that the Russian explorer, Otto von Kotzebue, got lost in them and longed for a good pilot to help him thread his way through. The channels were alive with beavers and river otters in fresh water, sea otters in salt water. And everywhere there were thousands and thousands of herons, curlews, sandpipers, dowitchers, and other shore birds.

The geese that wintered in the Bay Area were "uncount-able," according to Father Juan Crespi. An English visitor claimed that their numbers "would hardly be credited to anyone who had not seen them covering whole acres of ground, or rising in myriads with a clang that may be heard a considerable distance."

The environment of the Bay Area has changed drastically in the last 200 years. Some of the birds and animals are no longer to be found here, and many others have vastly diminished in number. Even those that have survived have (surprisingly enough) altered their habits and characters. The animals of today do not behave the same way they did two centuries ago; for when the Euro-peans first arrived they found, much to their amazement, that the animals of the Bay Area were relatively unafraid of people.

Foxes, which are now very secretive, were virtually under-foot. Mountain lions and bobcats were prominent and visible. Sea otters, which now spend almost their entire lives in the water, were then readily captured on land. The coyote, accord-ing to one visitor, was "so daring and dexterous, that it makes no scruple of entering human habitation in the night, and rarely fails to appropriate whatever happens to suit it."

"Animals seem to have lost their fear and become familiar with man," noted Captain Beechey. As one reads the journals and diaries, one finds the same observation repeated by one vis-itor after another. Quail, said Beechey, were "so tame that they would often not start from a stone directed at them." Rabbits "can sometimes be caught with the hand," claimed a Spanish ship captain. Geese, according to another visitor, were "so impudent that they can scarcely be frightened away by firing upon them."

Likewise, Otto von Kotzebue, an avid hunter, found that "geese, ducks, and snipes were so tame that we might have killed great numbers with our sticks." When he and his men acquired horses from the missionaries they chased "herds of small stags, so fearless that they suffered us to ride into the midst of them."

Von Kotzebue delighted in what he called the "superfluity of game." But one of his hunting expeditions nearly ended in disaster. He had brought with him a crew of Aleutian Eskimos to help hunt sea otters for the fur trade. "They had never seen game in such abundance," he wrote, "and being passionately fond of the chase they fired away without ceasing." Then one man made the mistake of hurling a javelin at a pelican. "The rest of the flock took this so ill, they attacked the murderer and beat him severely with their wings before other hunters could come to his assistance."

It is obvious from these early reports that in the days of the Ohlones the animal world must have been a far more immediate presence than it is today. But this closeness was not without drawbacks. Grizzly bears, for example, who in our own time have learned to keep their distance from humans, were a serious threat to a people armed only with bows and arrows. During his short stay in California in 1792, Jose Longinos Martinez saw the bodies of two men who had been killed by bears. Father Font also noticed several Indians on both sides of the San Francisco Bay who were "badly scarred by the bites and scratches of these animals."

Suddenly everything changed. Into this land of plenty, this land of "inexpressible fertility" as Captain La Pérouse called it, arrived the European and the rifle. For a few years the hunting was easy—so easy (in the words of Frederick Beechey) "as soon to lessen the desire of pursuit." But the advantages of the gun were short-lived. Within a few generations some birds and animals were totally exterminated, while others survived by greatly increasing the distance between themselves and people.

Today we are the heirs of that distance, and we take it entirely for granted that animals are naturally secretive and afraid of our presence. But for the Indians who lived here before us this was simply not the case. Animals and humans inhabited the very same world, and the distance between them was not very great.

The Ohlones depended upon animals for food and skins. As hunters they had an intense interest in animals and an intimate knowledge of their behavior. A large part of a man's life was spent learning the ways of animals.

But their intimate knowledge of animals did not lead to conquest, nor did their familiarity breed contempt. The Ohlones lived in a world where people were few and animals were many, where the bow and arrow were the height of technology, where a deer who was not approached in the proper manner could easily escape and a bear might conceivably attack—indeed, they lived in a world where the animal kingdom had not yet fallen under the domination of the human race and where (how difficult it is for us to fully grasp the implications of this!) people did not yet see themselves as the undisputed lords of all creation. The Ohlones, like hunting people everywhere, worshipped animal spirits as gods, imitated animal motions in their dances, sought animal powers in their dreams, and even saw themselves as belonging to clans with animals as their ancestors. The powerful, graceful animal life of the Bay Area not only filled their world, but filled their minds as well.

Abel Posse

The Dogs of Paradise

Abel Posse's THE DOGS OF PARADISE, *a* 1987 *Argentine novel, provides a cosmic and comic treatment of the voyage of Christopher Columbus to the New World—the voyage of a divine fool to a state of mystical awareness. In it, Posse hilariously jumbles historical realities.*

Through the centuries, Columbus's tragic fall, the image of the great discoverer returning to Spain in chains, has inspired many writers (among them Walt Whitman and Charles Olson, both represented here). In Abel Posse's portrait, Columbus is both a tragic figure and a fool, a divine fool at play in the fields of a godforsaken paradise.

Columbus's greatest failing from the Spanish point of view was an inability to govern. His rule on Hispaniola was a nightmare. Every imaginable atrocity was perpetrated on the native population, while the Spaniards fell to fighting amongst themselves. Columbus made a series of terrible decisions. His first settlement was at Navidad, so named because he had managed to sink his ship, the SANTA MARÍA, *on Christmas Eve there. Columbus dropped off a passel of sailors at this casually chosen site and returned to Spain. The undisciplined sailors behaved like savages, and the settlement was destroyed by natives.*

Columbus's next settlement was at Isabela, named for his queen and—at least in the literary imaginations of such writers as Alejo Carpentier and Salman Rushdie—mistress. There he began construct-

*ing an ambitious fortress city, surrounded by moats and parapets.
Unfortunately, this project took a heavy toll on his colonists, who had
spent eleven weeks living with the livestock on their voyage from the
Canary Islands. Soon Columbus was exacting tribute from the Americans and cutting off the hands of those who could not fill their quotas.*

*A group of Spaniards under the leadership of Francisco Roldán
revolted against Columbus and founded a new settlement. Columbus's
world was disintegrating around him. Finally, in 1499, Columbus
wrote a long, rambling letter to the king and queen complaining of a
conspiracy against him, and expressing faith that God would punish
those who opposed him. The weary king named Francisco de Bobadilla
the new governor, and sent him to arrest Columbus. Entering the harbor of Santo Domingo, the first thing Bobadilla saw was two gallows
on either side of the river, a Spaniard hanging from each.*

*"Bobadilla forgot his instructions to proceed slowly," explains
Carl Sauer, and, "moving in with the full authority that he com-
manded, sent [Columbus and his] brothers back to Spain in chains.
This angry and demeaning act is what he is remembered for in history.
Thus ended, ignobly for all concerned, the first Spanish government in
the New World."*

*The Spanish destroyed the dogs of paradise, although Posse might
not agree. Columbus had remarked on them. They were small animals,
raised to be eaten, and what most astonished the Spaniards was that
they couldn't bark. They were extinct even before the Taino Indians
were. But Posse would probably argue that they had been transmuted
into the packs of mongrel dogs that roam the streets of Latin American
cities today, for paradise, after all, is eternal.*

It was evident that the admiral had suffered a probably irrevers-
ible mutation. The rational consciousness characteristic of Occi-
dental "men of reason" had forsaken him.

Unconsciously, whether as self-punishment or self-acclaim,
he had been transformed into the first complete South American. Although he had not been born of carnal union between
races, he was the first mestizo. A mestizo without an umbilicus.
Like Adam.

Wise Taino elders and the *cacique* Guaironex analyzed the evolution—or involution—of that god from the sea who behaved differently from the rest of his companions from beyond the sea. They reasoned, correctly, that he would be the first human to live in the new cycle of the Black Sun.

This new creature lived in a state of apathy, without high expectations or explicit despair. Abandoned by Prometheus.

He surrendered completely to idle hours in his hammock. He ate what grew around him or fell from the trees, without a trace of nostalgia for red meat—or, in his case, pasta. What did he eat? Bananas, sweet potatoes, salted ants, quantities of coconut milk, mango juice.

His days were long and uneventful. Neither subsistence nor existence pried him from his hammock. A few yawns could occupy twenty minutes. By now he had lost all notion of time as he had known it!

In his mind, where rational corridors and cables had ceased to function, memory and reality, as in dreams, blended into a single continuum, so that verb tenses—past, present, and future—were lumped together in the oblivion of a grammatical museum.

The Taino shamans concluded that drugs were not indicated; his internal capacity for the secretion of delirium was perfect, perhaps a level as high as that of the poet-king Nezahualcoyotl. So in his case they omitted the *peyotl* and *ayahuasca* usually so effective in counteracting the brutalizing effect of reason.

The river of thought and dream flowing through the admiral's mind had taken on an American coloration. The black-and-white gothic landscapes of Castile illuminated by the light of human bonfires had been replaced by gentler images. When Anacaona appeared, the princess who with her unfortunate husband Caonabó had been carried back to Spain, her image invariably fused (again, the mestizo) with that of the unforgettable vision of Simonetta Vespucci as Venus in the Botticelli painting commissioned by Lorenzo the Magnificent. But Anacaona's legs were like two bow shafts stretching toward a central fire, and Simonetta's hair, the color of old gold, like the autumn dusk above the Arno.

Isabel walked by in the clothes she had worn at the siege of Granada, but against a background of palm trees. Then La Beltraneja with her bay percherons. Far in the distance, as if in the depths of time, Beatriz Arana, seated on a keg of leeches, awaiting her executioners.

All these figures from memory had in common a certain indolence: they stretched, they drowsed, they gazed at geraniums. Everything merged into synthesis or symbol (as in dreams), the years of terror in Castile reduced to black mantilla-draped shadows of women on their way to seven o'clock mass.

These are lethargic memories that lead neither to drama nor to historical grandeur. Even the fiery Beatriz Bobadilla appeared several times in the penumbra of the loveshrine, lying on her bed of snow-white fleece, but she is a blue-black panther with the green eyes that transfix her victim before she springs.

A new form of imagination is in gestation. The cinnamon skin of Siboney, the black flowers along tropical trails. The alleged perfidy of Anacaona.

The admiral passes carefree hours beneath the branches of the Tree of Life.

*   *   *

Las Casas set out along the ascending path Ulrich Nietz had exhausted days before. He was borne along on the wind of faith: he was seeking God in His essential invisibility.

He found the marble gates and other irrefutable traces of the One God. Item: a waterfall crashing on rocks below, producing a deafening roar and generating a mist with the seven primordial colors of creation. Item: a beetle with golden dots on its back. Item: a serpent with a clearly drawn Christian cross just below its head. Item: no fewer than a dozen gigantic butterflies dusted with the Vatican colors, a delicate yellow and a white like powdered sugar.

He had no doubts. He had found sufficient proof. He had

been trained to understand God from the aspect of absence. The presence of His great absence, to state it with the precision of the eminent men of the Church. He fell into a profound prayer of celebration and gratitude. On his knees in the mud, he endured a series of nocturnal downpours. A real drenching, but he was sustained by an inner warmth that kept his skin dry. The electric charge of faith.

In the depths of his soul he had heard the silence of God, grave and expressive.

He noticed that the sign of the petrified serpents was repeated in several stone ruins glimpsed through the lianas. Beyond the shadow of doubt, this was the symbol of God's fury toward the instrument of temptation. He found an enormous anaconda head, similarly petrified.

He had his evidence of the language and designs of God. God's fingerprints were more prominent here in this abandoned Paradise than anywhere in his creation. Even the most incompetent investigator would find overwhelming proof of the unmistakable will of the All-Powerful.

He returned more sure than ever of his pastoral mission. Now, shoulder to the wheel!

He passed by the Tree of Life, stopping only long enough to retrieve his cassock, wrinkled and faded by the rains. He barely greeted Landsknecht Swedenborg. The admiral was sleeping.

*   *   *

Death descended. Everything changed in Castile. The bells of Salamanca, Arévalo, Segovia, and Madrid tolled dolefully. Clappers muted in black cloth. Gray peals.

There had been somber news in the course of recent years. The plague of the Indies, syphilis, was rampant. Brothels had lost their medieval gaiety. Shameful pustules and chancres. Lead salts (the same treatment François I would recommend to Carlos V) were imported from the Hanseatic cities. The long era of venereal peril began, the curse of the body that would endure slightly longer than the Inquisition itself (until the discovery of penicillin).

Multiple misfortunes befell Fernando and Isabel; their first daughter, the Queen of Portugal, died, and also their grandson *don* Miguel. Juana, hypersensitive, married to Felipe the Handsome, was in the throes of a severe crisis; she was blind with jealousy. Half naked, beneath stormy skies, she had perched above the iron gate of the castle of Medina del Campo and refused to come down.

Torquemada died, and with him the empire lost the machinery of collective guilt. He lived seventy-five years of untiring redemptive cruelty. One morning he was found in his bed, inanimate, cold, covered in a thick powder of sperm. Successive layers of dried semen on his thighs, like sheets of mica, had turned into an odorless powder as his body heat evaporated. The clinging odor of French pissoir that accompanied him throughout his life had dissipated. A number of Catholic chroniclers, misled by the absence of stench, ventured to record that "he died in an aroma of sanctity."

But their greatest sorrow, their major misfortune, was the death of Prince Juan, the favorite son, the newly married heir, only twenty years old. The delicate and marvelous Prince Juan, educated in *belles lettres*, in holy war, in elegance.

The physical debility and delicacy of that son who had not inherited his parents' angelical terribleness had always terrified Isabel, but she had never thought he would die as he had, of love. Incapable of sustaining his erotic obsession for the beautiful Margaret of Austria.

He had grown so weak in the abuse of the gods that in the last months he lost all defenses against worldly reality: the glimpse of a hunchback or an ugly spinster was enough to bring on a fever. During a banquet he had fainted when the tenor missed the high notes of a *romanza*.

As Isabel was traveling to Medina del Campo to try to dislodge her daughter from above the gate, Fernando was informed of the serious illness of the prince, and he raced toward Salamanca without stopping at posthouses.

When he arrived, he realized that the proximity of death

had reversed normal roles: the prince was the father of his father the king.

"Father," Juan said to him. "I have known nothing but happiness, love, and gifts. Let us accept the will of God with humility."

The king wept silently, almost with a peasant's fathomless grief. He kissed the delicate hands of his exhausted, defeated son. He told him:

"My beloved son, you must answer now that God calls you. For He is above any other king, and has for you kingdoms and dominions greater than those that were yours or to be yours."

That night Pietro Martire wrote: "With his demise were lost the hopes of all Spain."

Death, in all its might and power, struck the queen, never to leave her. Her world whirled around her. She had to fall back toward the palace of medieval metaphysics from which she had fled with Fernando during the creative years of the parabola of the Renaissance. Her passion for the Earthly Paradise, and her faith in her body and the fiesta of action were mortally wounded.

When Fernando informed her of the worst news she could hear, she merely murmured:

"The Lord giveth and the Lord taketh away. Amen."

The adventure of the terrible adolescents was abruptly terminated. Isabel's face sagged; she was struck by illness: an insatiable thirst. She turned her back to the world and set her gaze on the realms of the beyond. She would grope her way through icy mists, desolate, searching for the face of her most beloved son, Prince Juan, already in the world of the dead.

It was the end of the sect of the seekers of the Earthly Paradise.

King Fernando passed from grief to resentment, as if he had been cheated or deceived. Devastated by sorrow, he spent hours meditating on the "curse of America." The figure of the admiral was never far from the horizon of his wrath.

As a distraction, he devoted furious energy to matters of state.

In a black mood, he studied all communications from the Indies, and listened to the slander and envy circulating in the court. He was informed about ordinances, the rebellion of Roldán, the concerns of the church hierarchy.

He had always considered Colón a mystic without temporal loyalties, an extremely dangerous species.

He brooded over the fact that because of him the New World was divinely interdicted, its arable lands covered by the cloak of God, a property owner who forbade use of his lands in his absence.

Worst of all, the admiral had had the gall to propose that the natives were angels. Not even slaves to be bought and sold. Fernando settled the matter: he declared that they were vassals, and capable of being converted to Christianity. That is, they were not divine property, nor chattel of the Spanish rabble that had confiscated them.

Then, with almost no delay, Fernando acted: he summoned Commander Francisco de Bobadilla and appointed him his plenipotentiary.

That same gray afternoon in Castile, amid the sound of muffled drums and the interminable litany from the chapel of ladies-in-waiting reciting the rosary with Isabel, he signed the order for the arrest of Colón and his men. It was March 21, 1499.

*   *   *

He surrendered peacefully. Any man who has passed the threshold of the Open is forever immune to the trivialities of the apparential world.

Colonel Roldán was clever enough to manipulate the temporary power of Commander Bobadilla (he yielded to his authority with the same tactical skill Hitler would employ centuries later with Marshal Hindenburg). He volunteered to command the party detached to the Tree of Life.

The admiral seemed unsurprised when he saw the party erupt from the jungle. They surrounded his hammock, kicking aside dozens of indifferent dogs that seemed accomplices to the lassitude of the gray-haired man who spent his days dozing beneath the Tree of Life.

"Your excellency, I arrest you under order of their majesties the king and queen." These were Bobadilla's only words.

His subordinates rushed forward. They clothed the admiral in a Franciscan robe, as if Colón's Arcadian nakedness were his most serious crime and constituted a criminal offense against public decency.

Rattle of chains and shackles. Quinteros and the cook Excobar had brought them in a box of irons. (Since the first days of the revolution, Padre Buil had generously placed at Colonel Roldán's disposition all the instruments of inquisitorial procedures. Ever since, in America, repression would have the profound flavor of redemptive, pastoral, exorcising torture.)

The admiral, patiently seated in the hammock, observed as they hammered the heavy fetters around his ankles. He marveled that they erred only once.

The march toward the coast was slow and humiliating. The secretary, who had kept the required record of events, attempted to make conversation with the royal paymaster to mask the sound of irons rattling with every step.

Colón's brother Bartolomé, secular head of government, was arrested along with all the other Colóns: cheesemakers, tailors, and weavers who were making their mark in commerce and industry.

His weary eyes, grown accustomed to the filtered light of the jungle, were dazzled by the brilliant light of the coast.

There was one principal street (which in time would be called Colón Boulevard). It led to the plaza and the cathedral, still mainly of logs but beginning to be sheathed with carved stones taken from the native pyramids and temples.

All along this main street, the crowd hurled insults:

"Admiral of gnats!"

"Impostor! Jew swine!"

Captive to the vision of boundlessness, he could not judge them. He felt neither meekness nor anger. Not even scorn.

During the time he had lain beneath the Tree of Life, *doing* had obviously powerfully consolidated itself. The Hegelian "man of reason" had implacably gained the upper hand. Everyone, including his relatives, was busily sacking Paradise.

The angels, scourged, emaciated, had been apportioned among the *encomienda* owners. Decimated by suicides and labor deep in the mines. Victims of progress. Forever severed from the soul of the world in which they had lived as brother to papaya and puma.

The admiral was disconsolate.

"Man destroys what he says he loves most," he murmured.

During that humiliating procession, he had come to realize that his civilized fellows feared nothing so much as a return to primordial harmony. That they had been diabolically diverted to find their pleasure in sorrow. That like most readers of Dante, they preferred Hell to Heaven.

It was clear: after a brief shock of the Ordinances, they were once again comfortably engaged in exploitation, the ardors of happiness, and the effort to hold decency above the countless temptations of vileness. It was a game, or a vice, guaranteed by Roldán's immutable order.

Nostalgic, nevertheless, on Sundays they purified themselves of weekday evil. Squarcialuppi and the brand-new crew of Italian priests reminded them from the pulpit of the blessings of Paradise. Exhorted them to be unconditional supporters of Good.

The admiral observed that in addition to the cathedral, many other buildings were being constructed of masonry or adobe. He marveled at the profusion of signs: Santángel Bank & Hawkins Ltd., Bologna Beauty Salon, Palace of the Inquisition (Semper Veritas), Cook Travel Agency, United Fruit Company, Castile Hotel, Sagardúa Buffet.

*   *   *

Then came the day no one could have imagined, nor been militarily prepared to respond to: the amazing revolt of the dogs.

It was a silent invasion. More passive resistance than assault.

An army of the diminutive dogs of Paradise (nostalgic for
Adam, the admiral and Landsknecht Swedenborg believed).
Undersized, voiceless beasts so undoglike that the first Spanish
chroniclers had even denied their genus, as Heidegger would
say, their "essence of dogness." Some described them as a
"species of edible rodents that do not bark but shriek if beaten."
These chroniclers did not suspect that their souls, absorbed
from dead or vanished masters, were guiding them toward the
Great All-Being after the alarms of life. (The Toltecs had sanc-
tified them and included them in the Calendar. Any dog might
be a *nahual*, the repository of a suffering human soul.)

The settlers watched them swarm down the dunes toward
the town, like a flowing mantle, unafraid of the fiercely barking
mastiffs or the shouts and musket fire of guards unable to stem
the canine tide.

They filled every corner of the town. They did not bite,
not even the children. They did not howl. All they did was uri-
nate wherever they could: walls, supplies, on any motionless
vertical surface (including the boots of the blind Landsknecht
Osberg de Ocampo, who never listened to what anyone was
telling him).

Insignificant, always denigrated, now in numbers they
formed a mammoth and formidable beast. Their enormous,
peaceful, silent presence was terrifying.

La Diabla closed the doors of her establishment and
gathered her pupils on the upper floors, in the Paris salon.

Shouts, cries, ringing swords. Young children galloping
madly about, crazy with joy once they learned the dogs would
not bite.

The dogs held the city in thrall for more than an hour.

By midafternoon they decided to retreat to the jungle.
Since that day, and for all time, these standard-bearers of nostalgia have declared rebelliousness through lack of action. They
did not fade into remote forests with the arrogance of the
jaguars, or flee to high treetops like the quetzals and delicate

orchids. Ever since, in silent packs, they have wandered field and town, from Mexico to Patagonia. Rarely, spurred by extreme hunger, they have attacked sheep and horses. (Stories of these episodic assaults abound in the vice-regal history of Río de la Plata and Nueva Granada. Once, after the turn of the twentieth century, the dogs even surrounded and cut off a small military fort.)

They are ubiquitous, these irrelevant creatures no kennel club would register.

The small disciplinary party headed by Colonel Roldán finally reached the coast.

As the admiral stepped into the yawl that would ferry him to the caravel of his deportation to Spain, he saw on the beach great piles of the carved marbles of the Gate. A chain of forced laborers up to their waists in water were loading the blocks. He lifted a hand to the son of the *cacique* Guaironex, and to the bearded rebel Mordecai, who was paying dearly for his ideas on redemption.

The carved stones, numbered with carbon according to the plan of the specialists who had dismantled the *zócalo*, were being shipped at the request of the Catholic University of Brussels, where a section of "Amerindian Archaeology" had already been opened and the stones of the Indian temple square would be installed.

The admiral looked toward the decimated palm grove that once had murmured a whisper of welcome; he saw the forced laborers and the large mustaches and gunbelts of Roldán and his men. He realized that America would remain in the hands of tinhorn dictators and autocratic *corregidores*, like the palace of his childhood, seized by lackeys who had known how to steal the arms for themselves.

Invincible, he murmured:

"Purtroppo c'era il Paradiso."

Charles Olson

He Lost the Indies to a Worm

Charles Olson, presiding spirit of the Black Mountain school of poetics, lived for a time in the Yucatán and studied Mayan culture in some detail. A collection of his letters ranging over the subject, published as THE MAYAN LETTERS, *was edited by his favorite correspondent, fellow poet Robert Creeley. Olson wrote to Creeley, "I have no doubt . . . that the American will more and more repossess himself of the Indian past."*

In this passage from THE MAXIMUS POEMS, *Olson, like Posse in the selection from* THE DOGS OF PARADISE, *views Columbus as a tragic, defeated figure (although Posse endows him with heroic dignity). But in Olson's view, Columbus was defeated not by elements within the Spanish community, but by the very world he had discovered; in Olson's image, Columbus was defeated by the teredo, a small wormlike mollusk that bored holes in the bottoms of the Spanish vessels. Columbus was careless, too hasty to spend the time in port necessary to remove them. And so the body of his work was shot through with holes and his vessels prone to shipwreck. The natural world of the Americas exacted a surprising revenge: the success of his earthshaking enterprise was consumed by worms!*

Respecting the earth, he sd,
it is a pear, or,
like a round ball upon a part of which there is a prominence
like a woman's nipple, this protrusion
is the highest & nearest to
the sky

      Ships
have always represented a large capital investment, and
   the manning,
the provisioning of same

               It was the teredo-worm
               was 1492: riddle a ship's hull
               in one voyage ("pierced
with worm-holes
like a bee-hive
the report was

               Ladies & Gentlemen,
               he lost his pearl,
               he lost the Indies
               to a worm

2
GODS & DEMONS
Native Views of the Encounter

You shall live in square houses, in a barren land, and beside those square houses you shall starve.

WATERDRINKER, Sioux prophet

Americans fleeing from Columbus. (1493)

The World Becomes Small

> Scattered through the world shall be the women who sing and the men who sing and all who sing. . . . No one will escape, no one will be saved. . . . There will be much misery in the years of the rule of greed. Men will turn into slaves. Sad will be the face of the sun. . . . The world will be depopulated, it will become small and humiliated.
>
> —MAYA: *The Book of the Books of Chilam Balam*

For the Europeans, the move to America was a marvel, a wondrous event that would lead to fantastic new discoveries, that might even see the prophecies of the ancients come to pass on this earth. The Europeans quickly realized that their world had changed forever—this was a new age, a new world.

The Americans also recognized the momentous nature of the change in their world, but had a very different vision of the future their encounter with the Europeans would produce. Without a concept of "America," as opposed to anywhere else, native Americans experienced a range of reactions: they welcomed the Europeans as their gods and their fate; they saw their arrival as a sign of doom, a cataclysm, the end of a historical cycle.

Their world was gone, and a new tragic world was beginning. But in time, with the forging of a new American mythos and a new appreciation of our multicultural society, the old ways would be reborn in new form: "Christopher Columbus," Gerald Vizenor has written, "landed in the New World with a striven western gaze that would be overturned in five centuries by the tribal people he saw as naked servants with no religion. . . . Columbus arises in tribal stories that heal with humor the world he wounded; he is loathed, but he is not a separation in tribal consciousness. The Admiral of the Ocean Sea is a trickster overturned in his own stories five centuries later."

Leslie Marmon Silko

The Invention of White People

Native American reaction to the discovery and conquest has survived largely through oral tales, through a tradition of storytelling. Leslie Marmon Silko writes: "White ethnologists have reported that the oral tradition among Native American groups has died out, because whites have always been looking for museum pieces and artifacts when dealing with Native American communities. . . . I grew up at Laguna listening, and I hear the ancient stories, I hear them very clearly in the stories we are telling right now."

"The Invention of White People" was published in Silko's book CEREMONY, *in* 1978. *It is a poem in the prophetic mode that tells the story of a new world created by the arrival of whites—a horrible vision of the most diabolical evil. The poem's anger and despair express the trauma of the conquest. The conquerors' practice of finding their own devil lying in wait for them in this new Eden finds its counterpart in the Indians' belief that they themselves had created their own demons, the white demons, by witchcraft.*

The old man shook his head. "That is the trickery of the witchcraft," he said. "They want us to believe all evil resides with white people. Then we will look no further to see what is really happening. They want us to separate ourselves from white people, to be ignorant and helpless as we watch our own destruction. But white people are only tools that the witchery manipulates; and I tell you, we can deal with white people, with their machines and their beliefs. We can because we invented white people; it was Indian witchery that made white people in the first place.

Long time ago
in the beginning
there were no white people in this world
there was nothing European.
And this world might have gone on like that
except for one thing:
witchery.
This world was already complete
even without white people.
There was everything
including witchery.

Then it happened.
These witch people got together.
Some came from far far away
across oceans
across mountains.
Some had slanty eyes
others had black skin.
They all got together for a contest
the way people have baseball tournaments nowadays
except this was a contest
in dark things.

So anyway
they all got together
witch people from all directions
witches from all the Pueblos
and all the tribes.
They had Navajo witches there,
some from Hopi, and a few from Zuni.
They were having a witches' conference,
that's what it was
Way up in the lava rock hills.
north of Cañoncito
they got together
to fool around in caves
with their animal skins.
Fox, badger, bobcat, and wolf
they circled the fire
and on the fourth time
they jumped into that animal's skin.

But this time it wasn't enough
and one of them
maybe a Sioux or some Eskimos
started showing off.
"That wasn't anything,
watch this."

The contest started like that.
Then some of them lifted the lids
on their big cooking pots,
calling the rest of them over
to take a look:

dead babies simmering in blood
circles of skull cut away
all the brains sucked out.
Witch medicine
to dry and grind into powder
for new victims.

Others untied skin bundles of disgusting objects:
dark flints, cinders from burned hogans where the
dead lay
Whorls of skin
cut from fingertips
sliced from the penis end and clitoris tip.

Finally there was only one
who hadn't shown off charms or powers.
The witch stood in the shadows beyond the fire
and no one ever knew where this witch came from
which tribe
or if it was a woman or a man.
But the important thing was
this witch didn't show off any dark thunder charcoals
or red ant-hill beads.
This one just told them to listen:
"What I have is a story."

At first they all laughed
but this witch said
Okay
go ahead
laugh if you want to
but as I tell the story
it will begin to happen.

Set in motion now
set in motion by our witchery
to work for us.

Caves across the ocean
in caves of dark hills
white skin people
like the belly of a fish
covered with hair.

Then they grow away from the earth
then they grow away from the sun
then they grow away from the plants and animals.
They see no life
When they look
they see only objects.
The world is a dead thing for them
the trees and rivers are not alive
the mountains and stones are not alive.
The deer and bear are objects
They see no life.
They fear
They fear the world.
They destroy what they fear.
They fear themselves.

The wind will blow them across the ocean
thousands of them in giant boats
swarming like larva
out of a crushed ant hill.

They will carry objects
which can shoot death
faster than the eye can see.

They will kill the things they fear
all the animals
the people will starve.

They will poison the water
they will spin the water away
and there will be drought
the people will starve.

They will fear what they find
They will fear the people
They kill what they fear.

Entire villages will be wiped out
They will slaughter whole tribes

Corpses for us
Blood for us
Killing killing killing killing.

And those they do not kill
will die anyway
at the destruction they see
at the loss
at the loss of the children
the loss will destroy the rest.

Stolen rivers and mountains
the stolen land will eat their hearts
and jerk their mouths from the Mother.
The people will starve.

They will bring terrible diseases
the people have never known.
Entire tribes will die out
covered with festered sores
shitting blood
vomiting blood.
Corpses for our work
Set in motion now
set in motion by our witchery
set in motion
to work for us.

They will take this world from ocean to ocean
they will turn on each other
they will destroy each other
Up here
in these hills
they will find the rocks,
rocks with veins of green and yellow and black.
They will lay the final pattern with these rocks
they will lay it across the world
and explode everything.

Set in motion now
set in motion

To destroy
To kill
Objects to work for us
objects to act for us
Performing the witchery
for suffering
for torment
for the still-born
the deformed
the sterile
the dead.

Whirling
whirling
whirling
whirling
set into motion now
set into motion.

So the other witches said
"Okay you win; you take the prize,
but what you said just now—
it isn't so funny
It doesn't sound so good.
We are doing okay without it
we can get along without that kind of thing.
Take it back.
Call that story back."

But the witch just shook its head
at the others in their stinking animal skins, fur
and feathers.
It's already turned loose.
It's already coming.
It can't be called back.

Popul Vuh

The Blinding of the Men of Maize

The creation myth of the Mayan civilization reflects its agricultural foundation. The POPUL VUH, *the Mayan sacred book, tells the story of the gods' attempts to create the human race. They tried to fashion people from such materials as wood and stone, but these creatures always possessed fatal flaws. Finally, the gods created the current race of people out of maize.*

In making the men of maize, the gods succeeded too well. The men of maize understood too much, and they had to be blinded or they would have challenged the gods themselves. The POPUL VUH *explains why ordinary "men of maize" cannot see the wisdom of the gods.*

The blindness of ordinary men justifies the role of priests and seers in Mayan society. Among the Maya, Aztecs, and other Americans, prophecies and oracles were the essence of wisdom, and so these societies were fatally dependent upon their priests and seers. They alone could interpret the signs that wouldn't yield their meaning to ordinary men. When the oracles failed to provide the wisdom required to respond to the threat of the Europeans, these societies were momentarily left without the mythic sense of direction needed to sustain their culture.

They had breath
> And existed.

And they could see too;
> Immediately their sight began.

They came to see;
> They came to know

Everything under heaven
> If they could see it.

Suddenly they could look around
> And see around

In the sky,
> In the earth.

It was scarcely an instant
> Before everything could be seen.

They didn't have to walk at first
> So as to gaze at what was under heaven:

They were just there and looked.
> Their understanding became great.

Their gaze passed over trees,
> Rocks,

Lakes,
> Seas,

Mountains
> And valleys.

Truly then
> They were the most beloved of men,

Jaguar Quiche,
> Jaguar Night,

Nought
> And Wind Jaguar.

And so then they came to see everything under heaven,
       And so then they gave thanks
To Former,
       And Shaper,
'Truly then twice thanks,
       Thrice thanks that we are created already,
And that we are mouthed
       And faced.
We can speak;
       We can hear;
We ponder;
       We move;
We think very well;
       We understand
Far
       And near,
And we can see large
       And small,
What is in heaven,
       What is on earth.'

They came to understand everything;
       They saw it:
The four creations,
       The four destructions
The womb of heaven,
       The womb of earth.
And not very happily
       Did they listen to this,
The Former
       And Shaper.

'It is not good
        What they say.
Aren't their names just formed
        And shaped?
But quite like gods
        Will they become then
Unless they begin to multiply
        And begin to grow numerous
When it whitens,
        When it brightens:
Unless it increases.
        Then so be it!'

And their eyes were chipped
        By the Heart of Heaven.
They were blinded like the clouding of the surface of a mirror;
        Their eyes were all blinded.
They could only see nearby then,
        However clear things might be,
And thus they lost their understanding,
        And all the wisdom of the four men
At the start,
        At the beginning.

Bernardino de Sahagún

Our Gods Have Died

There are fine contemporaneous accounts of the conquest of Mexico by Bernal Díaz, Francisco López de Gómara, and Diego Durán, and there are also various Indian accounts, which have been assembled by Miguel Léon-Portilla in THE BROKEN SPEARS: THE AZTEC ACCOUNT OF THE CONQUEST OF MEXICO. *But it is the work of Bernardino de Sahagún that has given us the fullest and truest—or at least the most sympathetic—portrayal of the Mexican participants and their culture.*

Sahagún, a Franciscan priest and professor of grammar, was born in Spain in 1499, and his recordings of native accounts are colored, certainly, by the attitudes of Spain. But he lived in Mexico from 1529 until his death in 1590, and he learned the Aztec language, Nahuatl. His initial goal was to propagate European culture, and indeed within ten years of his arrival in Mexico, the sons of defeated Aztec noblemen were composing heroic verses in Latin, under his instruction. But soon Sahagún had undertaken the project of recording Mexican myth and history in Nahuatl and appending translations to it. Thus of all the European chroniclers, it is through Sahagún that we most nearly approach the language (and thereby the mythos) of the conquered.

His most important work was HISTORIA GENERAL DE LAS COSAS DE NUEVA ESPAÑA (GENERAL HISTORY OF THE THINGS OF NEW SPAIN), *which attempted to record the linguistics and ethnographics of*

*Aztec society through a controlled survey of informants. The breadth
and depth of the document are unique in the era.*

In MEMORY OF FIRE: GENESIS, *Eduardo Galeano tells the story
of the seizure of this material by King Phillip II. After forty years of
gathering, recording, and translating native voices, Sahagún's life
work was confiscated by the king's command, for it was full of idolatry,
the devil's work. "The old native wise men offer their testimony to Fray
Bernardino de Sahagún: 'Let us die,' they plead, 'since our gods have
died.'" Sahagún refused to submit. "At eighty he clutches to his breast
a few papers saved from the disaster and dictates to his pupils in
Tlatelolco the first lines of a new work. . . ."*

*By good fortune, Sahagún's work was lost within the royal archives,
rather than destroyed as the king intended. The complete text has only
recently been published. This excerpt is a portion of an Aztec account of
the fall of Mexico by a resident of Tlatelolco (now a part of Mexico City).
The defiant Cuitlahuac, who succeeded Moctezuma and led the Aztecs
in heroic defeat when the cause was already lost, is said to have told
Moctezuma when the Spaniards first arrived: "I pray to our gods that
you will not let the strangers into your house." But Moctezuma and his
soothsayers read the signs differently. As Diego Durán writes of Moctezuma: "When he saw that the dreams were not in his favor . . . he
ordered the dreamers be cast into prison. After this no one wished to tell
his dreams to Moctezuma." The connections between gods and humans
had been severed and the Aztec leader conceded his power to the newcomers. Moctezuma's speech appears elsewhere in variant forms, but this
native account of it best conveys the psychological complexity of the
man, and his belief that the Spanish had been sent to inherit his rule.*

Moctezuma arrayed and attired himself to meet the Spaniards,
and he instructed his leading lords and princes, noblemen, and
governors to do so as well. Then they went to meet them. They
set out precious flowers in gourd containers: helianthus, talauma
mixed with popcorn flowers, yellow tobacco flowers, cacao blossoms. With more flowers they made wreaths and garlands.
They wore golden necklaces from which pendants dangled and
plaited neck bands.

Now Moctezuma met them in Uitzillan. He gave gifts to the commander: flowers, jeweled necklaces, garlands—he covered him with flowers, he wreathed his head with flowers. They had laid before him golden necklaces and all the gifts of greeting, which completed the meeting. He hung necklaces upon many.

Cortés said to Moctezuma: "It is you? Are you not he? Are you not Moctezuma?"

And Moctezuma replied: "Indeed yes, I am he."

With that he rose. He rose to meet Cortés face to face. He bowed deeply, drew him close, and straightened up.

And these words he spoke. He said to him, "O our lord, you have endured fatigue, you have borne great weariness. So have you come upon this earth. So have you come to the city of Mexico. You have come to lie upon your mat, to sit upon the seat that I have been guarding for you. Now the rulers have all left: Itzcóatl, Moctezuma the Elder, Axayacatl, Tizoc, Auitzotl, who only a moment ago was standing guard over you, who have come to govern the city of Mexico. Under those lords' protection your people were allowed to enter. Are they aware of it? If only one of them could see and marvel at what I am witnessing, what I alone see, in the absence of those lords! I am not dreaming, I am not viewing a vision in a dream, I am not gazing while sleeping—no, it is no dream that I am seeing you, that I am looking into your face. I have been afflicted for a long time now. I have looked off at that unknown place from which you came—from the clouds and the mists. And now this. The rulers who left said that you were coming to visit your city, that you would lie on your mat and sit on your seat. And now it has all been fulfilled. You have come, you have endured fatigue, you have borne great weariness. Peace be with you. Rest yourself. Visit your palace. Rest your body. Peace be with our lords."

When Moctezuma's speech was finished, Marina translated it to the Marquis. When he had heard Moctezuma's words, he spoke to Marina. He spoke to them in his rough words; in his tough language he said:

"Let Moctezuma be at ease and not be frightened. We love him much. Our heart is gladdened for knowing him and hearing him. Long we have wished to see him and look upon his face. And now we have done so. Now we have come to his home in Mexico. He will hear our words in time."

Aztec

Flowers and Songs of Sorrow

The earliest native accounts of the conquest are songs composed by surviving Nahuatl poets. They are collected in a document called the CANTARES MEXICANOS *in the National Library of Mexico. Nahuatl scholar Miguel Léon-Portilla calls them "among the first and most poignant expressions of '. . . the trauma of the conquest.' They reveal, with greater eloquence than the other texts, the deep emotional wound inflicted on the Indians by the defeat." This selection expresses the poet's view that the gods have turned their backs on the people of Mexico.*

Nothing but flowers and songs of sorrow
are left in Mexico and Tlatelolco,
where once we saw warriors and wise men.

We know it is true
that we must perish,
for we are mortal men.
You, the Giver of Life,
you have ordained it.

We wander here and there
in our desolate poverty.
We are mortal men.
We have seen bloodshed and pain
where once we saw beauty and valor.

We are crushed to the ground;
we lie in ruins.
There is nothing but grief and suffering
in Mexico and Tlatelolco, where once we saw beauty and valor.

Have you grown weary of your servants?
Are you angry with your servants,
O Giver of Life?

Octavio Paz

The Desertion of the Gods

The Aztecs were the strongest military power the conquerors encoun-
tered, and the Aztec defeat by the small group of Spaniards led by Her-
nán Cortés is the strange and fascinating story of their leader Mocte-
zuma's failure to act, a failure so abject it almost amounts to surrender.

This was the first great conquest to become a part of the collective
memory of the hemisphere. The eradication of the Caribbeans had been
a sordid and shameful affair that had left no American alive to tell the
tale. But in Mexico the Spaniards merely picked up the existing reins of
power. They built their churches on the foundations of Aztec temples
and played their games in Aztec ballcourts. Tenochtitlán (today Mexico
City) was still the government center of imperial power, but now the
power was Spanish. The Aztecs were not exterminated, but continued
their lives under the new government.

Mexico triumphed by assimilating the conquering Spaniards.
Cortés had a son by his native interpreter, La Malinche. The boy became
a symbol: the first mestizo, the first Mexican. Today many "Hispanics"
from Mexico and Central America more resemble the native Meso-
americans than they do the Europeans from whom the term is drawn.
So it is not surprising that Mexican writers have thought deeply about
the events of the conquest and their legacy through the centuries.

There are many theories for the strange behavior displayed by the

Aztecs upon the arrival of the Europeans. But it was clear that they recognized that they were entering a new age, a new world. They were barraged with troubling omens and portents. According to Nobel Prize-winning Mexican poet, essayist, and diplomat Octavio Paz, in this selection from THE LABYRINTH OF SOLITUDE, the Aztecs, shaken by a vision of cataclysmic change (and haunted by the guilt of being invaders into Mexico themselves), committed collective suicide.

Any contact with the Mexican people, however brief, reveals that the ancient beliefs and customs are still in existence beneath Western forms. These still-living remains testify to the vitality of the pre-Cortesian cultures. And after the discoveries of archaeologists and historians it is no longer possible to refer to those societies as savage or primitive tribes. Over and above the fascination or horror they inspire in us, we must admit that when the Spaniards arrived in Mexico they found complete and refined civilizations.

Mesoamerica—that is, the nucleus of what was later to be New Spain—was a territory that included the central and southern parts of present-day Mexico and a portion of Central America. To the north, the chichimecas wandered among the deserts and uncultivated plains. (Chichimeca is a generic term, without national distinctions, that was applied to the barbarians by the inhabitants of the Central Plateau.) The frontiers between were unstable, like those of ancient Rome, and the last centuries of Mesoamerican history can be summed up as the history of repeated encounters between waves of northern hunters—almost all of them belonging to the Náhuatl family—and the settled populations. The Aztecs were the last to enter the Valley of Mexico. The previous work of erosion by their predecessors, and the wasting away of the intimate springs of the ancient local cultures, made it possible for them to accomplish the extraordinary task of founding what Arnold Toynbee calls a Universal Empire, based on the remains of older societies. According to Toynbee, the Spaniards did nothing except act as substitutes, resolving through political synthesis the tendency toward dispersal that threatened the Mesoamerican world.

When we consider what Mexico was like at the arrival of Cortés, we are surprised at the large number of cities and cultures, in contrast to the relative homogeneity of their most characteristic traits. The diversity of the indigenous nuclei and the rivalries that lacerated them indicate that Mesoamerica was made up of a complex of autonomous peoples, nations and cultures, each with its own traditions, exactly as in the Mediterranean and other cultural areas. Mesoamerica was a historical world in itself.

In addition, the cultural homogeneity of these centers shows that the primitive individuality of each culture had been replaced, perhaps within a fairly recent period, by uniform religious and political structures. The mother cultures in the central and southern areas had in fact been extinguished several centuries before. Their successors had combined and re-created all that variety of local expression, and the work of synthesis had culminated in the erection of a model which, with slight differences, was the same for all.

Although historical analogies deserved the discredit they have suffered, it is almost impossible not to compare the Mesoamerican world at the beginning of the sixteenth century with the Hellenic world at the moment when Rome began its career of universal domination. The existence of several great states, and the survival of a great number of independent cities, especially in continental Greece and the islands, underscores rather than negates the prevailing cultural uniformity. The Seleucids, the Ptolemies, the Macedonians and many small and ephemeral states were not distinctive because of the diversity and originality of their respective societies, but rather because of the quarrels that fatally divided them. The same can be said of the Mesoamerican societies. In both worlds, differing traditions and cultural heritages mixed together and at last became one. This cultural heterogeneity contrasts strongly with the perpetual quarrels that divided them.

In the Hellenic world this uniformity was achieved by the predominance of Greek culture, which absorbed the Oriental cultures. It is difficult to determine the element that unified our indigenous societies. One hypothesis, valuable mainly as a theme for reflection, suggests that the role played by Greek culture in the ancient world was fulfilled in Mesoamerica by the great culture that flourished in Tula and Teotihuacán and that has inaccurately been called "Toltec." The influence of the cultures of the Central Plateau on those of the south, especially in the area occupied by the so-called Second Mayan Empire, justifies this idea. It is noteworthy that no Mayan influence has been found in the remains of Teotihuacán, whereas Chichén-Itzá was a "Toltec" city. Everything seems to indicate that at a certain time the cultural forms of central Mexico spread out and became predominant.

Mesoamerica has been described very generally as a uniform historical area characterized by the constant presence of certain elements common to all its cultures: an agriculture based on maize, a ritual calendar, a ritual ball-game, human sacrifices, solar and vegetation myths, etc. It is said that all of these elements originated in the south and were assimilated at various times by the immigrants from the north. If this were true, Mesoamerican culture would be the result of various southern creations that were adopted, developed and systematized by nomadic groups. But this scheme neglects the originality of each local culture. The resemblances among the religious, political and mythical conceptions of the Indo-European peoples, for instance, do not deny the originality of each one of them. But, apart from the particular originality of each culture, it is evident that all of them, because of decadence or debilitation, were on the point of being absorbed into the Aztec Empire, which was heir to the civilizations of the Central Plateau.

Those societies were impregnated with religion. The Aztec state was both military and theocratic. Therefore, political unification was preceded or completed by religious unification, or corresponded to it in one way or another. Each pre-Cortesian city worshiped gods who steadily became more alike: their names were different but the ceremonies honoring them were similar. The agrarian deities—the gods of the earth, of vegetation and fertility, like Tláloc—and the Nordic gods—celestial warriors like Tezcatlipoca, Huitzilopochtli and Mixcóatl—belonged to a single cult. The most outstanding characteristic of Aztec religion at the time of the Conquest was the incessant theological speculation that reformed, systemized and unified diverse beliefs, both its own and others. This synthesis was not the result of a popular religious movement like the proletarian religions that existed in the ancient world at the beginning of Christianity. It was the work of a caste located at the apex of the social pyramid. The systematizations, adaptations and reforms undertaken by the priestly caste show that the process was one of superimposition, which was also characteristic of religious architecture. Just as an Aztec pyramid often covers an older structure, so this theological unification affected only the surface of the Aztec consciousness, leaving the primitive beliefs intact. The situation prefigured the introduction of Catholicism, which is also a religion superimposed upon an original and still-living religious base. Everything was prepared for Spanish domination.

The conquest of Mexico would be inexplicable without these antecedents. The arrival of the Spaniards seemed a liberation to the people under Aztec rule. The various city-states allied themselves with the conquistadors or watched with indifference—if not with pleasure—the fall of each of their rivals, especially that of the most powerful, Tenochtitlán. But the political genius of Cortés, the superior techniques of the Spaniards (lacking in such decisive actions as the battle of Otumba), and the defection of vassals and allies, could not have brought about the ruin of the Aztec Empire if it had not suddenly felt a sense of weakness, an intimate doubt that caused it to vacillate and surrender. When Moctezuma opened the gates of Tenochtitlán to the Spaniards and welcomed Cortés with gifts, the Aztecs lost the encounter. Their final struggle was a form of suicide, as we can gather from all the existing accounts of that grandiose and astounding event.

Why did Moctezuma give up? Why was he so fascinated by

the Spaniards that he experienced a vertigo which it is no exaggeration to call sacred—the lucid vertigo of the suicide on the brink of the abyss? The gods had abandoned him. The great betrayal with which the history of Mexico begins was not committed by the Tlaxcaltecas or by Moctezuma and his group: it was committed by the gods. No other people have ever felt so completely helpless as the Aztec nation felt at the appearance of the omens, prophecies and warnings that announced its fall. We are unlikely to understand the meaning of these signs and predictions for the Indians if we forget their cyclical conception of time. As with many other peoples and civilizations, time was not an empty, abstract measurement to the Aztecs, but rather something concrete, a force or substance or fluid perpetually being used up. Hence the necessity of rites and sacrifices to reinvigorate the year or the century. But time—or, more precisely, each period of time—was not only something living that was born, grew up, decayed and was reborn. It was also a succession that returned: one period of time ended and another came back. The arrival of the Spaniards was interpreted by Moctezuma, at least at the beginning, not so much as a threat from outside than as the internal conclusion of one cosmic period and the commencement of another. The gods departed because their period of time was at an end; but another period returned and with it, other gods and another era.

This divine desertion becomes even more pathetic when we consider the youth and vigor of the nascent Aztec state. All of the ancient empires, such as Rome and Byzantium, felt the seduction of death at the close of their long histories. The people merely shrugged their shoulders when the final blow was struck. There is such a thing as imperial fatigue, and servitude seems a light burden after the exhausting weight of power. But the Aztecs experienced the chill of death in their youth, while they were still approaching maturity. The Conquest of Mexico is a historical event made up of many very different circumstances, but what seems to me the most significant—the suicide of the Aztec people—is often forgotten. We should remember that

▪▪

fascination with death is not so much a trait of maturity or old
age as it is of youth. Noon and midnight are the hours of ritual
suicide. At noonday everything stops for a moment, vacillating;
life, like the sun, asks itself whether it is worth the effort to go
on. At this moment of immobility, which is also the moment of
vertigo, the Aztec people raise their eyes toward the heavens:
the celestial omens are adverse, and the people feel the attrac-
tion of death.

> *Je pense, sur le bord doré de l'univers*
> *A ce goût de périr qui prend la Pythanise*
> *En qui mugit l'espoir que le monde finisse.*

One part of the Aztec people lost heart and sought out the
invader. The other, betrayed on all sides and without hope of
salvation, chose death. The mere presence of the Spaniards
caused a split in Aztec society, a split corresponding to the
dualism of their gods, their religious system and their higher
castes.

Aztec religion, like that of all conquering people, was a
solar religion. The Aztecs concentrated all their aspirations and
warlike aims in the sun, the god who is the source of life, the
bird-god who breaks through the mists and establishes himself
in the center of the sky like a conquering army in the center of a
battlefield. But the gods were not mere representations of
nature. They also embodied the will and desire of society,
which made itself divine in them. Jacques Soustelle has written
that Huitzilopochtli, the warrior of the south, "is the tribal god
of war and sacrifice... and his career begins with a massacre.
Quetzalcóatl-Nanauatzin is the sun-god of the priests, who consider voluntary self-sacrifice the highest expression of their doc-
trine of life and the world: Quetzalcóatl is a priest-king who
respects ritual and the decrees of destiny, refusing to fight and
dying in order to be reborn. Huitzilopochtli, on the contrary, is
the sun-hero of the warriors, defending himself and triumphing
in battle: he is the *invictus sol* who destroys his enemies with the
flames of his *xiucóatl*. Each of these divine personalities corre-

sponds to the ideal of some important segment of the ruling class."

The duality of Aztec religion, reflected in its theocratic-military division and its social system, corresponds to the contradictory impulses that motivate all human beings and groups. The death-wish and the will-to-live conflict in each one of us. These profound tendencies impregnate the activities of all classes, castes and individuals, and in critical moments they reveal themselves in complete nakedness. The victory of the death-wish shows that the Aztecs suddenly lost sight of their destiny. Cuauhtémoc fought in the knowledge that he would be defeated. The tragic nature of his struggle lies in this bold and intimate acceptance of fate. The drama of a consciousness that sees everything around it destroyed—even the gods—appears to preside over our whole history. Cuauhtémoc and his people died alone, abandoned by their friends, their allies, their vassals and their gods. They died as orphans.

The fall of Aztec society precipitated that of the rest of the Indian world. All the nations that composed it were overwhelmed by the same horror, which almost always expressed itself as a fascinated acceptance of death. Few documents are as impressive as the remaining handful that describe this catastrophe. Here is an expression of the suffering of the Mayas, as recorded in the *Chilam Balam de Chumayel*: "II Ahan Katun: the blond-bearded strangers arrived, the sons of the sun, the pale-colored men. Ah, how sad we were when they arrived!...The white man's stick will fall, will descend from on high, will strike everywhere....The words of Hunab-Ku, our one god, will be words of sorrow when the words of the God of Heaven spread out over the earth...." And later: "The hangings will begin, and lightning will flash from the white man's hands....The hardships of battle will fall upon the Brothers, and tribute will be demanded after the great entrance of Christianity, and the Seven Sacraments will be established, and travail and misery will rule this land."

B. Traven

A New God Was Born

The work of B. Traven, the radical recluse who was author of THE
TREASURE OF THE SIERRA MADRE *and numerous other novels and
story collections, combines irony and sympathy for the underclass. His
"A New God Was Born" is no exception. It tells of the Spanish arrival
on the Mayan island of Flores in Petén, the jungle lowland of
Guatemala. It is a classic tale of the meeting of two cultures, the misunderstandings that arise from the collision of their religions and beliefs.
The product of this encounter, Traven gravely assures us, might have
been "one of the greatest mysteries of mankind."*

A few years after Hernando Cortés had conquered Mexico, he
formed an expedition with the idea of discovering a seaway from
the Atlantic to the Pacific. For in that period of history the
Americas were believed to be huge islands and not one continental land mass extending from the Arctic to the Antarctic.

Cortés' expedition marched south with the hope of coming
upon a strait connecting the two great oceans. The farther south
they marched the more difficult became their situation, and
they were close to complete exhaustion when they arrived at the
great Lake of Petén, situated in what is today the Republic of
Guatemala.

On the islands of that lake and along the shores the expedition found many villages inhabited by Indians of the most hospitable and peaceful nature. They were the first human beings Cortés had met for weeks on his arduous march through the immense jungle, which stretched out for hundreds of miles to the west and to the east of the mighty Usumacinta River.

After its tedious march through tropical areas, where the trail had to be hacked out by Indian auxiliaries brought from Tlaxcala, the Cortés army was suffering from hunger and from all kinds of fevers and jungle diseases. The soldiers' bodies were covered with infected wounds caused by bites and stings of reptiles and insects. The expedition was considered even by its most optimistic officers to be a total loss. In its helpless condition, had it not come upon the hospitable natives of Petén, the so gloriously initiated enterprise would have ended in a huge disaster with no hope for any member of it ever to return to Mexico. Those Indians, had they been a warlike tribe, could have cornered and massacred the whole Cortés army.

(The expedition, by the way, was looked upon as a complete failure when it returned. It added little knowledge to what was known already. Its only achievement was its proof that, as far as it had ventured, there was no navigable strait between the Atlantic and the Pacific.)

The natives of Petén fed Cortés' men as they hadn't been fed since leaving the last populated region in Mexico many weeks before. They cured the sick and wounded, and they gave Cortés plenty of provisions so that the army could march without fear of hunger for the next few weeks.

In their fervor to please their uninvited guests even more and make them happier still, the Indian natives cheerfully agreed to be baptized by the visiting army. And so it was that all of them became good Christians.

The monks who accompanied the expedition saw to it that everything was done properly, according to the established rules. The peaceful natives appeared to have no objection to the destruction of their gods and images, to the cleansing of the Indian temples and the installing of new images brought by the strangers—images of the Holy Virgin, of Santiago, of San Antonio, and half a dozen more.

Because the monks hadn't time enough to baptize each native individually, they used another method. The baptismal ceremony was turned into a great fiesta, and all the natives of that region were directed to meet on a vast plain where their foreign guests would offer them a show such as they had never before witnessed.

They came, a thousand or so of them. They were asked to kneel down. Then the monks, with hands raised up as if in prayer, bestowed upon them the benediction and declared them Christians, good and true Catholics, who must obey their superiors in Rome.

Those kneeling near the monks, who had been touched personally upon their heads, were ordered to confer that touch upon any man or woman they were to meet.

Now the real show commenced. And what a show! Bugles and trumpets blared. Cannons and muskets were fired. Horsemen performed tournament feats, as knights used to do centuries ago.

These natives of Petén had never seen or heard cannons fired or trumpets sounded. Nor had they ever seen a horse before. So it was only natural that they believed every rider to be physically united to the steed he straddled. The fiesta was an awesome display of powers and happenings strange to the Indians. Of course they were confused. They saw the whole expedition army on their knees singing the *Te Deum*, the monks chanting and performing strange rites, the trumpets and bugles raised up and blaring, cannons and muskets spitting fire and thundering, and horsemen jousting and riding wildly upon the plain.

That whole show was such that even today anywhere on earth it would attract huge crowds and satisfy their craving for excitement. The natives received an impression which would live forever in their memories.

It was part of the clever policy of the conquistadores to impress natives with their power and make them believe that the white men of the expedition were gods of a kind. It was for that reason that it had been possible for such a ridiculously small number of Spanish soldiers to march on and on, leaving their rear unprotected, because the Indians whom they met on the way would never dare to raise arms against such divine beings.

Fortunately, those peaceful natives of Petén owned no jewelry of gold or silver, possessions which would have made the Spaniards believe the natives knew of gold and silver mines. To discover such mines and deposits had been the second reason—and for most members the first and only reason—that this costly expedition was undertaken. Nor did the Indians have pearls or precious stones. Not even the surrounding land was tempting to the Spaniards, who could lay their hands on better, more fertile properties in Mexico. The lake was the principal source of native income, an income which couldn't be earned just by loafing on the shore and looking dreamily across the water.

It was natural for Cortés to leave that unfertile area as soon as his army was well and on its feet again.

For all the services the Spaniards received from the natives they paid nothing. Cortés considered them well rewarded in that their sins (of whose existence the Indians formerly had known nothing) had been cleansed by the monks and all obstacles to their admission into heaven had been cleared away. In fact, Cortés left these people in a state of poverty such as they hadn't known for generations. He took full advantage of the Indians' natural generosity. All their stock of fruit, dried fish, dried meat, salt, medicinal herbs and roots, corn, chili, and cocoa beans (which served them for money) was carried off by the army for provisions.

On the day of his departure, however, Cortés decided to show the natives of Petén his gratitude by leaving them a royal gift. He presented them with a horse—which, as he well knew, would be accepted by them as the most precious payment they might have hoped to receive. The horse was of no further use to Cortés, since one leg was so badly injured and swollen that the poor animal would only have been a burden to the soldiers if taken on the return march. So it is a fact that this single sign of gratitude and generosity on the part of Cortés was given exclusively in his own interest.

The natives received the horse with all the excitement which such a kingly gift merited. Then the strange visitors disappeared as mysteriously as they had arrived. Had it not been for the horse they now possessed, and the vanished stock of food and supplies they no longer possessed, the peaceful hosts might have believed the whole adventure was a sort of mass hallucination.

Cortés had left a horse with the natives. What he, that mean trader, hadn't left with them was instructions on how to take care of that strange animal.

Now, every Indian the Spaniards met in peace or in battle since their arrival in America had always professed more fear of horses and horsemen than of cannons and muskets. The Spaniards were soon exploiting this fear and took the utmost care never to let Indians go near the horses in camp or at rest sites. Thus, Indians never got a chance to see horses fed. The Spaniards even spread the story that horses and horsemen were invulnerable. In those days horses and riders were heavily armored when in battle, and the Indians, with their primitive arms, couldn't kill or wound the horses or their riders. For this reason the Indians came to believe horses were war gods of a kind that they could never defeat. In the siege of Mexico City, however, this belief was badly shaken when Indians managed to kill several horses and their riders too.

The natives of Petén now had a horse. Word spread, and thousands came to see with their own eyes that strange creature the bearded white men had left behind in payment for services received. Because the exotic animal seemed related not only to the white men but also to the fire and thunder of cannons and muskets, the natives looked at the horse in constant awe. Soon they declared it a god.

They brought it the most beautiful flowers and the choicest fruit for gifts, just as they had brought offerings of flowers and fruit to their gods in the temples. The horse sniffed at the flowers in hopes of finding some fodder among them, for it had become very hungry since the conquerors' army had left.

The Indians noted this gesture of the horse and believed

that the animal had graciously accepted the offering. Yet, after sniffing the flowers, it turned around and stared longingly across the plain, where in the near distance a huge patch of the finest grass and fields rich with young green corn could be seen. But to these riches the horse couldn't go because it was firmly tied to a big tree.

The natives grew very sad, thinking they had offended this divine creature who refused to accept the flowers and fruit and turned its head aside in open disgust.

The oldest medicine man of the tribe was now sent for. He came, looked the horse over, and said: "You stupid tribesmen, can't you see that this godly being is very sick? Its leg is terribly wounded. See, it has a horrible lump there. Treat its ailments and it will be well again in no time, and then it will bless our lake, our fields, and our hunts."

It was then a custom with Indians, as it still is today in remote regions, to feed a sick person only wild turkey, in the belief, based on ages of observation, that the meat of the wild turkey has highly curative properties.

The horse's leg was doctored with mashed herbs and it was bandaged. This done, heaps of roast turkey, spiced with the finest aromatic vegetables, were arranged on large native jícara trays, decorated with flowers and fruit, and placed before the starving horse.

The poor animal, plainly at a loss as to how it was possible for human beings to be utterly ignorant of what a horse likes to eat, began to trample and shy about, trying harder and still harder to free itself from the rope so that it might reach the green pasture from where a light breeze brought the sweetest of odors to its quivering nostrils.

With every hour the horse grew more restless, started to dance about and neigh unceasingly until it tired itself out. Again the medicine man was called. Said he: "Well, you boneheads, don't you see what he needs?"

The natives understood. A beautiful young maiden was chosen, adorned, and offered to the horse. The horse, though, had no interest in this sacrifice either, and didn't even sniff at such a rare gift.

The poor natives by now couldn't think of anything to do to make the horse happy. It dawned on them that this divine creature was sinking fast, and their gloom turned to terror.

Here was a situation where a horse might have led a life so sweet, so quiet, and so happy, a life such as no horse had ever enjoyed since the time horses were found useful to man. Since the natives had no domesticated animals except a species of dog, all the rich pastures in the whole region would have been at the disposal of that horse, to be shared only by an occasional antelope. But ill luck had it that this horse with the heavenly prospects around it was destined to perish by starvation amidst plenty.

There was no remedy for these misunderstandings between the horse and the Indians. The horse finally could do nothing but lie down and die miserably, with a last hopeless glance of its bursting eyes upon that huge crowd of humans, among whom there was not one individual with horse sense.

Horror and consternation seized the natives when they found the horse stiff and cold and dead. Superstitious as they were, they naturally feared the revenge of that godly being.

What better could they do to protect themselves against the wrath of the foreign gods than to bestow upon the dead horse all the honors which a deity had a right to expect from frightened men?

With great ceremony, the horse was buried, and on top of its resting place a temple was built.

Ninety-three years later, in the year of Our Lord 1618, two monks of the Franciscan order came to Lake Petén carrying the gospel to the natives living there. Since Hernando Cortés had left the region no white man had visited Petén.

The two monks entered a temple with the intention of dethroning heathen gods and setting up in their place the image of the Holy Virgin.

Inside the temple their sight fell upon a huge sculpture in

stone, very crudely shaped. No matter which way they looked at it, there wasn't the slightest doubt that it was meant to be a horse. In the opinion of those monks the Indian artist had followed an inexplicable whim in making one of the horse's legs imperfect, exposing an ugly protuberance. Yet, from an artistic point of view, that imperfect horse leg was well done.

The monks had seen, heard, and read about very strange gods, but never had they expected to find a horse elevated to the highest worship, as this one was by the Indians of Lake Petén. That piece of sculpture was not only the natives' highest and most powerful creature god, but it was also their god of thunder and lightning, in whose honor, every year on a certain day, great celebrations took place.

The greatest surprise the monks received in their search of the temple, however, was a wooden cross so weather-beaten and decayed that they believed it to be easily a thousand years old. It was standing behind the stone horse and, according to the native folk tales, a white man with a long beard had either brought the cross or made it from a mahogany tree there in the area.

The monks' report on this strange find reached Spain and the rest of Europe and caused immense excitement among scientists and historians. The most fantastic speculations arose to explain the origin of that cross in such strange connection with the stone image of a horse, on a continent where, to the best knowledge of scholars, no horses had existed and no Indians would know anything of the shape or appearance of horses.

Just as speculations and theories had reached the stage where learned men seriously began to maintain that one of the apostles had come in person to the Americas during the first century, a certain registrar to the crown who was studying the archives of former Spanish kings stumbled upon a short note in one of the letters which Hernando Cortés had written to his sovereign, Emperor Charles the Fifth.

This note, relating the episodes of the so-called Hibneras Expedition, cleared up the event of the horse-god and the cross. Without the note, it would have remained one of the greatest mysteries of mankind.

3
CHILDREN
& CANNIBALS
Images of Americans

Bah! They don't wear breeches.

MICHEL DE MONTAIGNE

American domestic life. (1505)

They Lost the Sun

Rigid beneath the sheets, Mancio Serra de Lehuízamo un-
burdens his conscience. Before a notary he dictates and swears.
"That we discovered these realms in such condition that there
was not in all of them one thief, one vicious man, nor was there
an adulterous or bad woman . . ."

Pizarro's old captain does not want to depart this world
without saying for the first time: "That the lands and mountains and mines and pastures and hunting grounds and woods
and all manner of resources were governed or divided in such
a way that everyone knew and had his property, without anyone else occupying or taking it . . ."

Don Mancio is the last survivor of the army that conquered Peru. Over half a century ago he was one of those who
invaded this sacred city of Cuzco, pillaged the treasures of its
tombs and houses, and axed down the walls of the Temple of
the Sun so clotted with gold that their resplendences made
anyone who entered look like a corpse. He says he received the
best part of the booty: the immense golden face of the sun,
with its fiery rays and flames, which had dominated the city
and blinded the people of Cuzco at the hour of dawn.

Don Mancio wagered the sun at cards and lost it in a night.

—EDUARDO GALEANO,
"He Says He Had the Sun (Cuzco, 1589),"
in *Memory of Fire: Genesis*

European chroniclers of American exploration quickly experienced the same sense of loss that the Indians suffered. Into the
undifferentiated paradise they discovered, they soon introduced
distinctions, starting with the distinction between good and bad
Indians. At first Columbus viewed the Indians he found on the
islands of the Caribbean as innocents, as children in an unspoiled
garden. But they were naked; how then could they be people?
Very shortly he began portraying them as godless cannibals,
doing the devil's work. In the end, he would consider them a resource, no different from livestock.

The meeting of the Europeans and the Americans was a rare case of the encounter of peoples almost completely unknown to each other. Marco Polo's journey to the East, incredible as it seemed to his countrymen, was a progression through traveled lands, and explorers in Africa or Asia trailed rumors and reports of other peoples. But little prepared Americans and Europeans for their encounter.

Are they like us? Are they people? Are they gods? Are they beasts?

Early explorers struggled to form an estimation of the natives they encountered. Theorist Tzvetan Todorov, in *The Conquest of America*, describes the dilemma of the explorer: "Either he conceives the Indians . . . as human beings altogether, having the same rights as himself; but then he sees them not only as equals but also as identical, and this behavior leads to assimilationism, the projection of his own values on the others. Or else he starts from the difference, but the latter is immediately translated into terms of superiority and inferiority (in his case, obviously, it is the Indians who are inferior)."

According to Todorov, the conquest initiated a radical change in the Western mentality, a tendency to try to assimilate other cultures, to eliminate difference and reduce the sense of strangeness. Todorov believes that this period is now coming to an end, to be replaced by a new multicultural society: "We want *equality* without its compelling us to accept identity; but also *difference* without its degenerating into superiority / inferiority."

Carlos Fuentes

This Is America

"The world was so recent that many things lacked names and in order to indicate them it was necessary to point . . ." So Gabriel García Márquez describes Macondo, his fictional Colombian town in ONE HUNDRED YEARS OF SOLITUDE, *a novel that can be seen as a history of individual consciousness, the history of a country and a continent.*

In this essay Mexican writer Carlos Fuentes starts from Gabriel García Márquez's notion of naming to consider the uses of language in the invention of America, its land and people. The Spanish confronted with the marvelous American continent saw its natives as children, but they themselves were like children: to communicate, they had to point; to possess themselves of the New World, they had to name it. And Fuentes sees that for the Spanish, the "urgency of naming and describing the New World . . . is immediately related to this newness, which is, in effect, the most ancient trait of the New World."

This is America. It is a continent. It is big. It is a place discovered to make the world larger. In it live noble savages. Their time is the Golden Age. America was invented for people to be happy in. You cannot be unhappy in America. It is a sin to have tragedy in

America. There is no need for unhappiness in America. America does not need to conquer anything. It is too vast. America is its own frontier. America is its own utopia.

And America is a name.

Gabriel García Márquez is the name of an American writer, a writer of the New World that stretches from pole to pole rather than from sea to shining sea.

America is a name. A name discovered. A name invented. A name desired.

In his classic book *The Invention of America*, the Mexican historian Edmundo O'Gorman maintains that America was invented rather than discovered. If this is true, we must believe that, first of all, it was desired and then imagined. O'Gorman speaks of Europeans who were prisoners of their world, prisoners who could not even call their jail their own.

Geocentrism and scholasticism: two centripetal and hierarchical visions of a perfect, archetypical universe, unchangeable—yet finite because it was the place of the Fall.

The response to this "feeling of enclosure and impotence" was a hunger for space that quickly became identified with a hunger for freedom. Some of the names of this hunger are Nicholas of Cusa and later Giordano Bruno, Luca Signorelli and Piero della Francesca, Ficino and Copernicus, Vasco da Gama and then Columbus. Some of the names of this freedom in its European and America incarnations are:

First, the freedom to act on what is. This is the freedom won by Machiavelli in Europe and acted on by Cortés in America. It is the freedom of an epic world made to the measure of the self-made man, not he who inherits power but he who is capable, with equal measures of will and virtue, of winning it. This is the world, in the Latin American novel, of the descendants of Machiavelli and Cortés in the jungles and plains of the American continent: the Ardavines, the ferocious political bosses of the Venzuelan llanos, in Rómulo Gallegos; Pedro Páramo, the fissured Mexican cacique, in Juan Rulfo; Facundo, Sarmiento's immortal portrait of the archetypical caudillo. And: Francia,

Estrada Cabrera, Porfirio Díaz, Juan Vicente Gómez, Trujillo, and Somoza in the news; and in the novel, Asturias's El Señor Presidente, Carpentier's El Primer Magistrado, Roa Bastos's El Supremo, and, outliving them all, incorporating them all, García Márquez's ageless Patriarch:

"The only thing that gave us security in earth was the certainty that he was there, invulnerable to plague and hurricane... invulnerable to time."

The second is the freedom to act on what should be. This is the world of Thomas More in Europe and of Vasco de Quiroga in America. Discovered because invented because imagined because desired because named, America became the utopia of Europe. The American mission was to be the other version of a European history condemned as corrupt and hypocritical by the humanists of the time. On the contrary, Montaigne in France, Vives in Spain, and the Erasmists all over, saw in America the utopian promise of a New Golden Age, the only chance for Europe to recover, eventually, its moral health as it plunged into the bloody Wars of Religion.

Historically, Father Vasco de Quiroga, the Spanish reader of More's *Utopia*, lived in Mexico in the sixteenth century, arriving only a few years after the Conquest, and created communities totally faithful to the precepts of the English writer. Quiroga— venerated to this day by the Tarascan Indians as "Tata Vasco"— believed that only the utopian commonwealth would save the native inhabitants of America from violence and desperation.

He established the first utopian communities in Mexico City and Michoacán in 1535. That same year, Thomas More was beheaded by order of Henry VIII. So much, one would say, for utopia.

Yet utopia persisted as one of the central strains of the culture of the Americas. We were condemned to utopia by the Old World. What a heavy load! Who could live up to this promise, this demand, this contradiction: to be utopia where utopia was demolished, burned and branded and killed by those who wanted utopia: the epic actors of the Conquest, the awed band of sol-

■■■

diers who entered Tenochtitlán with Cortés in 1519 and discovered the America they had imagined and desired: a New World
of enchantment and fantasy only read about, before, in the
romances of chivalry. And who were then forced to destroy what
they had named in their dreams as utopia.

So Carpentier's narrator in *The Lost Steps* follows the Orinoco
River upstream, to its sources, to the Golden Age, to utopia, to

> this living in the present, without possessions,
>   without the chains
> of yesterday, without thinking of tomorrow . . .

And so the Buendías found a precarious Arcadia in the jungles
of Colombia, where not only the virtues of the Golden Age of
the past are acclaimed but also those of the coming Utopia of
Progress. We realize in García Márquez that, since the Enlight-
enment, Europe is the utopia of Latin America: law and science
and beauty and progress were now a Latin American albatross
hung around the neck of Europe: we expected from the West the
photograph that finally fixed our image for eternity; or the ice
that burns as it cools. But this notion of progress—and the names
that accompany it—is to prove illusory:

> "It's the largest diamond in the world."
> "No," the gypsy countered. "It's ice."

This gypsy lead us to the third aspect of freedom at the root
of the name America: the freedom to preserve an ironical smile,
a freedom not unlike that won by the first Spanish philosopher,
the Stoic from Córdoba, Seneca, but even more rooted in the
Renaissance reflection on the duality of truth and on the difference between the appearance and the reality of things. To deny
any absolute, be it the absolute of faith before or of reason now;
to season all things with the ironic praise of folly and thus
appear a madman in the eyes of both Topos and U-Topos: this is
the world of Erasmus in Europe and especially in Spain, where
Erasmus became, more than a thinker, a banner, an attitude, a
persistent intellectual disposition that lives to this day in Borges
and Reyes, in Arreola and Paz and Cortázar.

Indeed, Erasmus is the writer of the samizdat of Spanish and Spanish-American literature, the underground courier of so many of our attitudes and words, he who failed externally in Spain only to be victorious eternally forever and ever: Erasmus the father of Don Quixote; the grandfather of Tristram Shandy and Jacques le Fataliste; the great-grandfather of Catherine Moreland and Emma Bovary; the great-uncle of Prince Myshkin; and the revered ancestor of the Nazarín of Pérez Galdós, the Pierre Ménard of Borges, and the Oliveira of Cortázar—but also of the Buendías, who incessantly decipher the signs of the world, those that are put on trees and cows so their names will not be forgotten, or their functions, those signs they have seen behind the world's appearances, those they have read in the chronicles of their own lives, feverishly naming things and people and then feverishly deciphering what they themselves have written. What they have discovered—invented—imagined—desired—named.

> Macondo . . . was built on the bank of a river of clear
> water that ran along a bed of polished stones, which
> were white and enormous, like prehistoric eggs. The
> world was so recent that many things lacked names and
> in order to indicate them it was necessary to point . . .

The invention of America is indistinguishable from the naming of America. Indeed, Alejo Carpentier gives priority to this function of the American writer: to baptize things that without him would be nameless. To discover is to invent is to name. No one dare stop and reflect whether the names being given to things real and imagined are intrinsical to the named, or merely conventional, certainly not substantial to them. The invention of America occurs in a pre-Socratic time, that time whose disappearance Nietzsche lamented; it happens in a mythical time magically arisen in the midst of the nascent Age of Reason, as if to warn it, in Erasmian terms, that reason that knows not its limits is a form of madness.

García Márquez begins his Nobel Lecture by recalling the fabulous things named by the navigator Antonio Pigafetta as he accompanied Magellan on the first circumnavigation of the globe:

He had seen hogs with navels on their haunches, clawless
birds whose hens laid eggs on the backs of their mates,
and others still, resembling tongueless pelicans, with
beaks like spoons. He wrote of having seen a misbegot-
ten creature with the head and ears of a mule, a camel's
body, the legs of a deer and the whinny of a horse. He
described how the first native encountered in Patagonia
was confronted with a mirror, whereupon that impassioned giant lost his senses to the terror of his own image.

This discovery of the marvelous because it is imagined and desired occurs in many other fantastic chroniclers of the invention
of America; but even the more sober, one feels, had to invent in
order to justify their discovery of, even their being in the New
World. The pragmatical Genoese, Christopher Columbus, thinks
he can fool the Queen who sent him off at great expense, by
inventing the existence of gold and species where they do not
exist. When at last he does find gold—in Haiti—he calls the island
La Española, says that there all is "as in Castile," then "better
than in Castile," and finally, since there is gold, the gold must be
the size of beans, and the nights must be as beautiful as in Andalusia, and the women whiter than in Spain, and sexual relations
much purer (to please the puritanical Queen and not frighten off
further appropriations), but there are Amazons as well, and
sirens, and a Golden Age, and a good, innocent savage (to please
the Queen this time by amazing her). Then the good Genoese
merchant reasserts himself: the forests of the Indies where he
has landed can be turned into fleets of ships.

So we are still in the East. America has not been named, although its marvels have. Columbus has named what he was sent
to find: gold, species, Asia. His biggest invention is finding
China and Japan in the New World. For Vespucci, however, the
new thing about the New World is its newness. The Golden Age
and the Good Savage are here, described and named by him in
the New World, as a New Golden Age and a New Good Savage
bereft of history, once more in Paradise, discovered before the
Fall, untainted by the old. Indeed, we deserve Amerigo's name:
he invented our imaginary newness.

For it is this sense of total newness, of primeval appearance, that gives its true tone to names and words in America. The urgency of naming and describing the New World—of naming and describing in the New World—is intimately related to this newness, which is, in effect, the most ancient trait of the New World. Suddenly, here, in the vast reaches of Amazonian jungle, the Andean heights, or the Patagonian plains, we are again in the very emptiness of terror that Hölderlin spoke of: the terror that strikes us when we feel so close to nature that we fear we shall become one with her, devoured by her, deprived of speech and identity by her; yet equally terrified by our expulsion from nature, our orphanhood outside her warm maternal embrace. Our silence within. Our solitude without.

Jean Raspail

The End of the Earth Was Inhabited

Ferdinand Magellan, recognizing that South America was indeed a continent, proposed to reach the Spice Islands by sailing west and passing the continent to the south. He set sail from Seville, Spain, in 1519. It was a disastrous expedition. He found himself brutally suppressing a mutiny and dealing with imposing Patagonian Indians his chronicler Pigafetta matter-of-factly called "giants." Passing through the fearsome Strait of Magellan, his crew was reduced to eating hides, sawdust, and rats. Two years after he had set sail from Spain, Magellan finally reached the Phillipines, accomplishing the first circumnavigation of the globe. There he was murdered by members of his crew.

Jean Raspail's WHO WILL REMEMBER THE PEOPLE . . . *is a recent French novel based on the encounter between the Americans and the Europeans. Raspail, an explorer as well as an author, tells the story of Magellan's encounters with the Patagonian Indians and with Lafko, a representative of the Alacaluf people who called themselves the Kaweskar. The Kaweskar were a nomadic people, perhaps the first to arrive in America from Asia (and hence the oldest Americans of all), who settled in the Strait of Magellan at the extreme southern tip of the continent. They were small, bowlegged, and thick-lipped, in contrast to the generously proportioned Patagonians. In this selection Magellan's sailors ponder the humanity of the Patagonian Indians, as well as that of the elusive Kaweskar.*

The startling conclusion of this passage expresses the shock of the discovery of the Other, the realization that one is not alone.

In this southern winter of the year 1520, it still required four degrees of south latitude and a remarkable telescoping of fate before Lafko's canoe, adrift in the Stone Age, could meet Magellan's caravels in the second narrow of the great Strait—an encounter that would trigger something comparable to the splitting of the atom in Lafko's primitive brain. It also required four months, time for everyone to emerge safe and sound from this hell of snow and wind endured in almost total darkness and in an end-of-the-world solitude. Three hundred nautical miles apart, 340 miles undisturbed by a single living soul, two small groups of fires flickered pathetically, like dying stars struggling to pierce the endless night. Magellan was wintering at Puerto San Julian, an uninhabited and barren gulf on the Patagonian coast. Lafko was roaming with two other clans between the first two narrows in the eastern reaches of the Strait.

Magellan had raised a cross on a wind-buffeted dune. The first of a long series, it was blessed by chaplains blue with cold. The seamen were terrified. The drop in the temperature had struck them like a divine curse. No man had ever sailed so far south. Twenty years earlier, Vasco da Gama had rounded the point of Africa at the thirty-fifth parallel south. God had barely forgiven him for it. These men were at the forty-ninth parallel, and there was no strait in sight. Why did this continent refuse to end? The wind had laid the cross low and they had raised it again. Was that not a sign? An order to flee at once and head back to Seville, calling on God for forgiveness? The admiral had quelled two mutinies, turned several seamen over to the executioners, and clapped one captain in irons.

Now the very earth was freezing. The soil cracked open as if from underground explosions. Ice sheathed the rigging. Sails splintered like glass. In September they were still there. Fresh water was rationed. The ship's biscuits were hard as stone. Salt meat rotted, and whenever they were able to kill a seal, its greasy flesh made the sailors ill. They became anemic; their skin was covered with sores. Their teeth fell out. Some, incapable of digesting anything, starved. Others died of sorrow or discouragement. All were distressed at their inability to adapt morally and physically to conditions that Lafko—but he did not know it—had been overcoming for over five thousand years with all the arrested resources of his stubborn intelligence.

For a time the appearance of Patagonians in the camp distracted the sailors. To these small-statured Latins, they looked like giants, like a species of big monkey clad in animal skins that wrapped around their feet and legs and left tracks like those of a bear in the snow. Their women were big and fat, with enormous sagging breasts that aroused unhealthy laughter. They came from inland, and approached the shore only with terror and revulsion. Water was not their element. They were not the people of the canoe pictured by Behaïm and designated by Magellan as "Your Majesty's first subjects." Were they even human? To find out, they captured one who let himself be dragged off, terrified, while the others fled to watch the scene from a distance. They taught the name of Jesus to the giant, who repeated it in a huge voice, then the Paternoster, which he recited with frightened eyes but without skipping a single word. They made him kneel at the foot of the cross, where the chaplain baptized him and christened him Juan. They gave him a coat and trousers to wear, they set a hat on his head, and gave him bells, which he tinkled foolishly as he went off to join his tribe. Magellan shrugged. The crew laughed without comprehending the darkness of the scene they had just witnessed. The chaplain praised the Lord. To each according to his estate: prince, pauper, priest. The result was not long in coming. They heard horrible noises. It was Juan, dying, slaughtered and cut up by his fellows. The others continued to prowl around the strangers' camp, fascinated by their own fear, devoured by curiosity. The females with their enormous breasts made the crew restive. There were clashes, with deaths on both sides, and astonishing couplings between these women-mountains on all fours and these pale Christians, the spearhead of the West, humping upright in the snow like goats, their breeches round their ankles. The children born later from these unions would be smothered by their mothers as soon as the umbilical cords were cut . . .

From then on, the Patagonians would retreat behind a cloud of arrows and vanish from the landscape, herding their monstrous females before them like cattle. The sailors fell back into their moral torpor, as if these women had taken away with them what was most human in their souls. Two prisoners remained in the camp, two savages Magellan intended to present to the King of Spain. Refusing all nourishment, they quickly allowed themselves to die.

The days grew longer. The cold bit less savagely. The admiral gave orders to prepare to weigh anchor. One of the five ships was lost, driven on to the rocks by a storm. Another fled back to Spain to spread word of the admiral's madness: Locked in his room aboard the *Trinidad*, he sat face to face with the terrestrial globe, contemplating it for hours, the only one aboard who still stubbornly believed in it. On the heads of his assembled crews Magellan had sworn, "I will not turn back before the seventy-fifth parallel!" Which meant, "Beyond death . . ." The mutinies began again. The head of a second captain fell on the block that had served for all the previous executions. Fifty-eight years later, facing down a mutiny triggered by similar causes in this same Puerto San Julian, Sir Francis Drake would order the supreme penalty to be carried out on the very same block, found lying on the shore, still bloodstained. No trace of the cross remained . . .

Three ships continued the journey: *Concepción*, *Victoria*, *Trinidad*. The admiral's iron will had triumphed over every obstacle and all opposition. In the name of the King? That was mere appearance. In the name of imagination, which always invents a pretext for itself, since the most gifted of men grow bored between the past and the future, between memory and intuition, and burn to hasten the course of events. Perpetual motion. The dazzling flight forward. . . . To find out what was happening on the other side of the known, right up to the day when the other side would erupt with the thunder of divine anger . . .

Which was exactly what Magellan's men feared—the punishment awaiting them just around that ominous headland looming through the rain squalls. It was surrounded as far as the eye could see by reefs and breaking seas and clouds of spray flying heavenward like white ghosts. Fifty-two degrees south . . . Another storm roared in. Yardarms toppled and killed men. Keels shrieked against underwater rocks. Enormous seas combed the decks, buckling capstans, shattering boats. Anchors were swept away. The admiral had himself lashed to the foot of the mizzenmast beside the helmsman, similarly bound. Inside the three ships it was hell. The crews' quarters were awash with floating gear and ruptured barrels that bounced from bulkhead to bulkhead, mowing down everyone in their path. Sailors plugged their ears to shut out the awful crashing of waves against the hulls. The chaplain crawled across the decks, granting absolution to one man after another. A powerful current surged out from the distant headland, driving the enormous seas even higher and sweeping the small squadron out to sea, the ships cascading down the slopes of waves as if dropping into bottomless wells. Magellan's officers begged him to give up, to retreat, to turn back once and for all. But the admiral—the sternest, most poker-faced man in the world—was smiling! Drenched, numb to the marrow, his sickly frame shot through with pain, gazing out at a devastated fleet beyond help and thousands of leagues from Spain, he was smiling. He gave an order. Five colored flags in Spanish naval code fluttered to the masthead. The message was read aboard the *Concepción* and the *Victoria* in funereal gloom: "Two more hours. Keep in sight." An hour went by. Three flags rose: "One more hour." The admiral was still smiling. He had identified this cape. He recognized this current. It was the tide race Martin Behaïm had depicted on his terrestrial globe in Nuremburg at the very mouth of his *Passage to the Great Western Sea*. Within the hour it would change direction and carry them in toward the Strait . . .

Four hours later, and almost a flat calm. Floating in the lee of the headland, now within clear sight of the three ships as they rode the current westward inside what appeared to be a gulf walled in on all sides by mountains . . . Pigafetta, the *Trinidad*'s historian, noted in his journal: "Without the knowledge possessed by the admiral, who would have dreamed of seeking out a channel here . . . ?"

The place was utterly deserted. The only sounds were the roar of the seas and the cries of big black cormorants wheeling curiously over the *Trinidad*. Forms like reclining giants stirred on the rocks. They were only sea lions, which soon dived to safety. No trace of human life. They had lost sight of the fleeter *Concepción* and *Victoria*, which had gone on ahead to reconnoiter the inner reaches of the gulf. Suddenly a cannon boomed to westward, where they had last been seen. Then another, echoed by the mountains, its reverberations rolling from cliff to cliff through the solitude. Now the solitude had been violated—it was victory! The two caravels had found the entrance to the first narrow. The crew wept with joy. The admiral fell to his knees. It was All Saints Day. If this strait led him to the solution of the enigma, the admiral vowed, he would christen it *Estrecho de Todos los Santos*. The name never caught on, and the Strait would forever be known by Magellan's name.

The headland he christened *Cape of the Eleven Thousand Virgins* because of the thousands of submerged rocks at its feet, which gave it a retinue of dancing spray, of eternally fluttering white veils. Today it is called Cape of the Virgins.

For Lafko it had no name. It could have no name. It was a mythical place where the Kaweskar canoes never ventured. Glimpsed only rarely from afar, on unnaturally clement days, it marked the outer limits of a world beyond which nothing existed. You could not name the inconceivable . . .

Yet it was from this *inconceivable* that Magellan's ships sailed in.

From the bows of two longboats, pilots cautiously sounded the first narrow, mile by mile, before the squadron moved in behind them. Looking up to take their bearings from dry land, they made a grim discovery. Its back to a cliff wall, a corpse stared out at them with dead eyes. It was the corpse of a stunted man with short bow legs, long ink-black hair, a sloping forehead, slanting eyes, and a short flat nose above a wide, thick-lipped mouth. He was very ugly, and he was beginning to rot. Around him a ring of red-painted sticks had been stuck into holes in the rock. Weapons lay at his feet—a sharpened stick, a stone club, a bone harpoon. His name was Taw, father of Lafko. The sailors crossed themselves, and hastened onward.

The end of the earth was inhabited!

Juan de Matienzo

They Are Built to Serve

Spanish jurist Juan de Matienzo, in his GOVERNMENT OF PERU, *made this judgement on the humanity of the Indians, whom he described as pusillanimous, timid, fearful, weak, and stupid. In this brief passage, notice how his argument for their servitude resembles those used later to justify the American slave economy.*

Indians are naturally born and raised to serve. And it can be known that this is what they were born for because, as Aristotle says, such types were created by nature with strong bodies but less intelligence. So it can be seen that the Indians are physically very strong—much stronger than the Spaniards—and can bear more than they can, for they carry burdens of twenty-five to fifty pounds on their backs and walk along beneath them without difficulty. . . .

The stronger they are, the less intelligence they have.

Garrison Keillor

The Savage Ojibway

In this selection from LAKE WOBEGON DAYS, *Garrison Keillor deftly satirizes the European penchant for seeing the Americans as "savages."*

The first white person to set foot in Lake Wobegon and claim credit for it was either Father Pierre Plaisir in 1835 or Count Carlo Pallavicini the following year, depending on whether Father Plaisir set foot here or much farther to the west. According to his own calculations, he was near Lake Wobegon (or Lac Malheur, as the voyageurs called it), but the terrain he describes in his memoir, *Le Monde* (1841), seems to be to the west, perhaps as far as Montana. The mountains he says he saw were not any of ours.

He and his six *amis* had come to the New World to gain *gloire* and *bonneur* through *nouveaux exploits* despite *les dangers*, but instead got lost and spent June and July looking for the route back to where they had come from, the Northeast Passage. When they made camp at Lac Malheur, if that is where they were, their confusion was complete and their leader was suffering from *abominable abdominale*. He was *misérable* even before he lay down to sleep in the grass and the *muskitos* attacked him.

He had observed in his journal that "these are big vicious *muskitos*, not like our French insects," but that was before they got serious. A cloud of them descended after dark, and he lay and suffered for a while, then yelled, "*J'expire! Je quitte!*" and tore into the underbrush. His friends shouted, "*Courage, mon père!*" and ran after him. Their footsteps made him think his *ennemis* were coming, and he dashed west in *terreur* for some distance until he was captured by the Ojibway. They looked on it as protective custody, but when Father Plaisir returned to France and wrote his book, he described them as savages and said the country was a wilderness and he would never go back. He forgot that he had never been invited.

Michel de Montaigne

On Cannibals

One of the wryest—as well as most eloquent and persuasive—rebuttals of arguments against the humanity of the Americans was by Montaigne, "the inventor of the essay." Like Matienzo, he begins by citing Aristotle. He discusses the reports of a land like paradise. He also raises the specter of cannibalism, which was rare in the Americas, but a powerful force in the European imagination. Montaigne concludes that "we may indeed call these new peoples barbarous if we judge them by the rule of reason. But not if we judge them by ourselves, who outstrip them in every sort of barbarity."

For a long time I had a man staying with me who had spent ten or twelve years in that other world, discovered in this century, where Villegaignon landed [Brazil]. This discovery of an un-bounded land seems to me worthy of consideration; I'm not sure that another world might not some day be found, since so many wiser men than we were mistaken about this one. . . .

    He was a plain and simple man, and thus better than others for giving true evidence; for sophisticated men, though they ob-serve more, and better, are always laying interpretations upon what they see, and in order to give weight and credibility to their interpretations they can't resist stretching matters a bit. They never describe things just as they are but always bend them and

cloak them with their own point of view; and to make their judg-
ments even more credible and attractive they are not loath to add
a little to the telling, to embroider and embellish their tale.
Whereas my guest is a truthful man indeed, or one so simple
that he lacks the art of building up and coloring his fictions, and
one who is wedded to no theory. Such was my man, a man who
has, moreover, brought a number of sailors and traders by to see
me, whom he had met on his voyage. I shall therefore be satisfied with what he told me, and not consult the cosmographers
about it. . . .

From what I have heard, then, about this nation, I can see
nothing barbarous or uncivilized about it, except that we call
barbarism anything that does not conform to our own customs.
We have no other standard of truth and reason but the example
and model of the opinions and usages of the country where we
live. There we always find the perfect religion, the perfect government, the perfect and most refined way of doing all things.
The people of that land are wild in the sense that we consider the
fruits that nature has produced on her own and in her ordinary
progress to be wild; whereas in truth it is the ones we have altered
artificially and diverted from the common order that should be
considered wild. In the former we still see in full life and vigor
the genuine and most natural and useful virtues and properties,
which we have bastardized in the latter, adapting them only to
please our corrupt tastes. And yet in some of the uncultivated
fruits of those countries there is a delicacy of flavor that is excellent even to our taste and rivals that of our own fruits. It is not
reasonable that art should gain the point of honor over our great
and powerful mother Nature. We have so overburdened the
beauty and richness of her works with our inventions that we
have quite smothered her. And yet, whenever she shines in her
purity she marvelously puts to shame our vain and trivial efforts—

Uncared, unmarked, the ivy blossoms best;
In desert rocks the ilex clusters still;
And sweet the wild bird's untaught melody.
                        —PROPERTIUS

With all our efforts we are unable to challenge the nest of even the smallest of birds in its texture, beauty, and convenience; nor even the web of the poorest spider.

All things, says Plato, are produced either by nature, by chance, or by art: the greatest and most beautiful by one or other of the first two; the least and most imperfect by the latter.

These nations, then, appear to me barbarous only in the sense that their minds conform to their original simplicity. They are still ruled by the laws of nature and have hardly been corrupted by ours; rather, they still live in such a state of purity that I sometimes regret that they were not known in an earlier time when there were men who could have appreciated them better than I can. . . .

Theirs is a nation without commerce, with no knowledge of letters, no science of numbers, no offices of law or politics, no use for slaves, no wealth or poverty, no contracts, no inheritances, no divisions of property, no occupation except idleness and no kinship other than brotherhood, no clothing, no agriculture, no metals, no use of wheat or grain. There are no words in their language for falsehood, treachery, dissimulation, avarice, envy, detraction, or pardon.

These people live in a region with a most agreeable and temperate climate, so that, according to my witnesses, a sick man is seldom seen. They assure me they never saw a native shaking with palsy, with dripping eyes, toothless, or bent with age. Their country lies by the sea and stretches about a hundred leagues inland to high and lofty mountains. They have great abundance of fish and flesh, which bear no resemblance to ours, and which they eat roasted, without any other preparation. The first man who took a horse there, although he had visited there several times before, so horrified them when on his mount that they shot him dead with arrows before recognizing him. . . .

They rise with the sun and immediately eat their only meal for the day. They do not drink with their meal, like some other Eastern peoples of whom Suidas tells us, who drank apart from eating; but they drink several times a day, and to excess. Their drink is made of some root; it is of the color of our claret wines, and they only drink it warm. This beverage will keep only two or three days; it has a slightly pungent taste, is not heady, and is good for the stomach, though laxative for those who are not used to it, while a most pleasant drink for those who are. In place of bread they eat a white material resembling preserved coriander. I have tried some of it and found it sweet but rather tasteless.

The whole day is spent in dancing. The younger men hunt animals with bows. Some of the women meanwhile spend their time warming their drink, which is their chief duty. In the morning before they begin to eat, one of the old men preaches to the whole barnful of people, walking from one end to the other, repeating the same words several times, until he has completed his round (for the buildings are at least a hundred paces in length). He repeats only two themes, valor against enemies and love to wives (an obligation they never fail to mention, with the refrain, "It is they who keep our wine warm and seasoned."

In several places—my house, for one—we can see the form of their beds, their ropes, their wooden swords and the bracelets with which they cover their wrists in battle, and large canes hollowed out at one end by the sound of which they keep time in their dances. They are close-shaven all over, and remove their hair much more neatly than we do, although their razors are only made of wood or stone. They believe that the soul is immortal, and that those who have served the gods well are lodged in the part of the heaven where the sun rises, and the damned in the west. . . .

They wage wars with the nations beyond their mountains, farther back on the mainland, going to battle quite naked, with no other weapons but bows or wooden swords pointed at one end, after the fashion of the tongues of our boar-spears. It is marvelous with what obstinacy they fight their battles, which never end but in massacre or bloodshed: for of routs and terrors they know not even the meaning. Each man brings back as a trophy the head of the enemy he has slain, and fixes it over the entrance to his dwelling. After treating his prisoner well for a considerable time, and giving him all that hospitality can devise, the captor convokes a great gathering of his acquaintance. He ties a cord to one of the prisoner's arms, holding him at some distance for fear of being hurt, and gives the other arm to be held in the same way by his best friend; and these two, in the presence of the whole assembly, dispatch him with their swords. This done, they roast and eat him in common, and send bits of him to their absent friends. Not, as one might suppose, for nourishment, as the ancient Scythians used to do, but to signify an extreme revenge. . . .

I take no issue with our denouncing the barbarity of such acts, but I regret that in judging their errors we should be so blind to our own. I think there is more barbarity in eating a live than a dead man, in tearing on the rack and torturing the body of a man still full of feeling, in roasting him piecemeal and giving him to be bitten and mangled by dogs and swine (as we have not only read but seen in recent memory, not between old enemies but between neighbors and fellow citizens, and, what is worse, under the cloak of piety and religion), than in roasting and eating him after he is dead. . . .

We may indeed call these new people barbarians if we judge them by the rule of reason, but not if we judge them by ourselves, who outstrip them in every kind of barbarity.

Their warfare is entirely noble and large-spirited, and is as fair and excusable as can be expected in that human scourge, their only motive being a zeal for valor. They do not strive to conquer new territory, for they still enjoy that luxuriance of nature which provides them, without labor and pains, with all necessary things in such abundance that they have no need to enlarge their borders. They are still in that happy state of not desiring more than their natural needs demand: anything beyond that is superfluous for them.

They generally call each other, if of the same age, brothers; if younger, children; and the old men are fathers to all the others. These latter leave to their heirs in common the full and undivided possession of their property, without any but that pure title that nature gives to her creatures, by bringing them into the world. . . .

Three men of that nation, not knowing how dearly it will one day cost them in tranquillity and happiness to know the corruptions of this side of the world, and that this intercourse will be the cause of their ruin (which indeed I imagine is already advanced—poor wretches, to be allured by the desire to see new things and to leave their own serene sky to come and see ours!) were at Rouen at a time when the late King Charles IX was there. The king had a long talk with them. They were shown our ways, our pomp, the form of a fine city. Then somebody asked what they found most marvelous. They mentioned three things, the third of which I am sorry to have forgotten, but I still remember two. They said that in the first place they thought it quite strange that so many big men with beards, strong and armed, who were about the king (they were probably thinking of the Swiss who formed his guard) should submit to obey a child, rather than choosing one of their own number to command them. Second, they observed that some men among us were gorged full with all kinds of good things, while their halves (they have a way of speaking of men as if they were halves of one another) were begging at their doors, emaciated with hunger and poverty; they thought it strange that these necessary halves could suffer such injustice, and that they did not seize the others by the throat, or set fire to their houses.

I had a long talk with one of these men, but I had an interpreter who followed my meaning so badly, and was at such a loss, in his stupidity, to take in my ideas, that I could get little satisfaction out of him. When I asked the native, "What do you gain from your superior position among your people?" he said it was "to march foremost in war." How many men did he lead? He pointed out a stretch of ground, to signify as many as that space could hold: it might be four or five thousand men. Did all his authority lapse with the war? He said that one thing remained: when he visited the villages that were dependent on him, they made paths through their thickets for him, by which he might pass at his ease.

None of which sounds too bad—but, bah! they don't wear breeches.

Alejo Carpentier

Seven Americans Discover Spain

*One of the more memorable incidents in the life of Columbus is his pre-
sentation of his New World booty to Isabella on his return from the voyage of discovery. Whatever Columbus's true mission—there is some
question whether the intention was to reach the Indies or to discover and
claim new lands—it was a commercial enterprise, and not altogether a
cheap one. Columbus returned to Spain with a vision of a new world
(one that he perfected with practice) but little of certain value to be
entered into the ledger books. Consequently, as Eduardo Galeano tells
it in his own version of the incident in* MEMORY OF FIRE: GENESIS,
*"Hostile murmurs are heard in the salon. The gold is minimal, and
there is not a trace of black pepper, or nutmeg, or cloves, or ginger; and
Columbus has not brought any bearded sirens or men with tails . . ."*

*Columbus biographer Gianni Granzotto gives the story an emo-
tional telling in* CHRISTOPHER COLUMBUS: THE DREAM AND THE
OBSESSION, *in which Columbus's appearance at the royal court was a
complete success: "Amid all that majesty," he writes, "the Indians stood
half-naked, painted, and according to Lope de Vega, bozados—'muz-
zled.' A page carrying a trayful of gold bars circulated among the
guests. Another went around with the wicker cages containing parrots
with green and yellow feathers. Ferdinand and Isabella's eyes filled with
emotion as they listened to Columbus describe his adventures in that*

■■■

*winning, eloquent voice of his. When Columbus raised his eyes from
time to time, he encountered Isabella's gaze. She seemed to be bursting
with joy, and the gentle smile that Columbus thought he saw rise to her
lips bore a hint of tenderness, ever so slight."*

*Cuban Alejo Carpentier has a different idea about the parrots.
Unequaled at depicting pomp and ceremony, he begins his account—a
selection from his last novel,* THE HARP AND THE SHADOW (1979)—
*with the triumphant Columbus entering the royal palace "like a trader
who enters a castle with a magnificent exhibition." His exhibition is
called "The Spectacle of the Marvels of the Indies." Although he has not
returned with riches in gold, his presentation is rich with allusions to
Ophir, the golden land Solomon seeks in* GENESIS, *and Colchis, the land
of Jason's Golden Fleece. But, as the seven wide-eyed American captives
watch in astonishment, Columbus's orchestration of his performance
goes slightly awry, and the scene threatens to turn to farce.*

*Later we learn from Diegito, one of the captives, the Americans'
opinion of Spain.*

Under the brilliant April sun, the peerless city of Seville welcomed me like a conquering prince returned from the grandest
victory, with joy and jubilation, with banners and bells, with
compliments showering down and tributes from the balconies,
with the music of organs and the trumpets of heralds, the bustle
of a Corpus Christi procession, and the noise of flutes and bag-
pipes and oboes. And after the rejoicing and fiestas and the ban-
quets and the balls, I received my greatest reward: a letter from
Their Highnesses inviting me to court, which was in Barcelona
at this time of year, and—even more important to me—directing
me to start immediately to organize a new voyage to the lands I
had discovered. Caesar entering Rome in a triumphal chariot
could not have felt more proud than I! Reading between the lines
of the letter, I thought I saw the satisfaction and praise of one
who considered my achievement, in some sense, as a token of
victory placed at the feet of his Lady by a knight, a hero like
those whose deeds are celebrated in romances ... Impatient to
see her again, it didn't take any more than that for me to start off,

with my boxes of trophies, those parrots that were still alive—a bit runny-nosed and lackluster after their long trip, I had to admit—and, especially, my little band of Indians. Though I must say that those Indians, their eyes full of hate, were the only cloud—black cloud—casting a dark shadow on the vast horizon stretching toward the west that had just been opened up for me again, and much more safely this time. For of the ten captives we had taken, three were at death's door, and the physics that cure us—clysters, sweet drinks, suppositories, and leeches—do not help these men, who are prostrated by a cold, in agony, the life departing from them in fevers and shakes. For these three, it was quite obviously too late for the apothecary; it was that morbid hour when one must fetch the carpenter. As for the others, they seemed to be heading in the same direction, although their faces still brightened a little when I brought them a good jug of wine—something I was careful to do both morning and night. And the problem isn't that they drink constantly to get drunk—which helps them bear the inevitable pain they feel because of their exile from their country—rather it's that feeding them creates a difficult problem. To start with, they consider milk from a goat or a cow to be the most disgusting beverage any man could taste, they are amazed that we swallow this animal fluid, good only for nursing the beasts that fill them with misgivings and even fear, because before we came they had never seen these beasts with horns and udders, which are not found on their islands. Dried beef and salt fish repel them. They find our fruits repugnant. They spit out cabbage and turnips, and even the most succulent stews, claiming they're inedible. They like only garbanzo beans, because they taste a little, but only a little—according to Diegito, the only one we have managed to teach a few words of Spanish—like a food from their country, *maize*, a few sacks of which I have carried along, but which I've always scorned, not considering it fit for civilized people, though it might, perhaps, be good enough for pigs and asses. For all that, I think wine, although they have grown all too fond of it, can sustain them through their stubborn fast and give them strength for the new journey that was now planned. But that still left the question of the clothes for their presentation to the sovereigns. Out of respect for Their Majesties, they couldn't appear in court almost naked, the way they did in their own nation. And if they dressed the way we did, they wouldn't look that different from certain Andalusians with tan complexions—or from Christians mixed with Moors, of which we have a few in Spain. Luckily, at this critical moment, I was visited by a Jewish tailor I had met the year before near the Puerta de la Judera in Lisbon, where he had a shop, and who now, having gone from circumcised to Genoan—like so many others!—found himself in the city. He advised me to put them in red breeches sewed with little gold threads ("That's it . . . Perfect!" I said), loose shirts that expose their chests, which are smooth and hairless, and, on their heads, head-pieces like tiaras, also of gold thread ("That's it . . . Perfect!" I repeated, "As good as gold"), filled with exquisite feathers—although not from the birds on their islands—that drape gracefully down the backs of their heads, over their black manes, which grew quite a bit during our voyage, and which I would now have to wash and curry like the coat of a horse, on the morning of the day of the presentation.

And the day arrived. All Barcelona was celebrating. Like a trader who enters a castle with a magnificent exhibition, I entered the palace where she awaited me, followed by the fabulous company that would perform the Spectacle of the Marvels of the Indies—first spectacle of its kind ever presented in the great theater of the universe—a company that I left in the bedroom, in an order determined several days before when I directed the rehearsals and arranged the characters. Escorted by heralds and ushers, I entered Their Majesties' throne room, slowly, solemnly, with the tread of a conqueror, without losing my poise or being dazzled by the splendor of the ceremony or the applause that greeted me—particularly pleasing was the sound of the applause of the many who were now repenting ever having been my enemy. My compass and beacon, on this walk down the crimson carpet that led straight to the royal platform, was the face of my sovereign, illuminated at this moment by the most ineffable smile. After I kissed the royal hands, she bade me take a seat— me, the renowned Genoan, the Genoan with hidden roots and ancestry that I alone knew—between Castile and Aragon; the grand entrance door opened again and, walking two by two, carrying them on high, the porters brought in my trophies. On large silver trays—very large to make my display seem more impressive—the GOLD: chunks of gold, almost as large as a man's hand; delicate gold masks; gold figurines, devoted, no doubt, to some idolatry that for now I was very careful to keep quiet; little beads of gold; nuggets of gold; tiny plates of gold— not as much gold, to tell the truth, as I had hoped: gold that sud- denly seemed too little gold, much too little gold, next to the jewels, the coats of arms, the embroidery that whirled around me, the gold tapestries, gold maces held by bearers, the gold borders of the canopy—too little gold, when all was said and done. Just the first glint of gold, behind which, far off in the dis- tance, one can glimpse more gold, and more gold, and more gold. . . . But now the Indians were entering—summoned by the cap- tain who blew the lion-tamer's whistle that was used to tell them to do this or that—and on their hands and arms and shoulders they carried all the parrots that were still alive, more than twenty—all tremendously agitated by the movement and voices of those present for this occasion; besides, before the procession of marvels from across the sea made its entrance, I had given them many crumbs soaked in red wine, which made them raise such a hubbub that I was afraid they would suddenly start talk- ing, repeating the bad words they had certainly heard on board the ship and during their stay in Seville. And after the Indians knelt down in front of Their Majesties, howling and sobbing, palsied, frenzied (begging the sovereigns to free them from the captivity in which I had enchained them, to return them to their homelands, although I explained that they were thrilled, trem- bling with joy, at being prostrate before the Spanish throne . . .), some of my sailors came in, carrying the skins of snakes and lizards, larger than any found here, and branches, dried leaves, and withered vegetation, which we displayed as examples of valuable spices, although nobody was really looking at them, all eyes were fixed on the prostrate Indians—who were still sobbing and howling—and on the green parrots who had started to vomit cheap red wine all over the royalties' red carpet. Seeing that the spectacle was starting to get out of control, I sent the Indians out with their birds, and the sailors with their plants, and I got to my feet, facing Their Majesties, and showing my profile to the brilliant assembly that filled the room—which, I have to admit, was suffocatingly warm, and full of the sour smell of sweat-soaked silk, satin, and velvet—and I began to speak. I spoke slowly at first, describing the drama of the voyage, our arrival in the Indies, our encounter with its inhabitants. To describe these new lands, I evoked the beauty of Spain's most celebrated regions, the sweetness—I knew what I was doing—of the fields of Córdoba, although I certainly moderated my tone when I compared the mountains of Hispaniola with the summits of Teide. I told of seeing three sirens, on the ninth day of January, in a place where there were numerous tortoises—ugly sirens, to tell the truth, and with the faces of men, not the beautiful, musical temptresses I had seen, like Ulysses (what a whopper!) off the coasts of Malagueta. Since it's easy to keep on talking once you get started, I gradually became inspired by my own words, enlarging my gestures, stepping back to allow my voice to resound, listening to myself as I would to somebody else, and the names of the most splendid lands, both real and fabled, began to roll off my tongue. Every gleaming, glistening, glittering, dizzying, dazzling, exciting, inviting image in the hallucinatory vision of a prophet came unbidden to my mouth as if impelled by a diabolical interior energy. Without my willing it, Hispaniola was transfigured by this inner music, so that it no longer resembled Castile and Andalusia, oh no! it grew, it swelled, until it achieved the fabulous heights of Tarsus, of Ophir or Ophar, and finally reached the borders, which I had found at last—yes, found!—of the fabulous kingdom of Cipango. And there, in that very place, was the incredibly rich mine mentioned by Marco

Polo, and I had come to announce the fact to this kingdom and to all of Christendom. Colchis, Land of Gold, had been found, not in a pagan myth this time, but in its consummate reality. And gold was noble, and gold was good: *Genoans, Venetians, anyone who has pearls, precious stones, anything of great value, they all are willing to travel to the ends of the world to trade, to exchange these things for gold; gold, the greatest good; gold, the greatest treasure; whoever has gold can have anything in the world and can even attain paradise* . . . And with this voyage of mine, this amazing voyage of mine, the prophecy of Seneca has been fulfilled. Now . . .

> *Venient annis*
> *saecula seris quibus Oceanus*
> *vincula rerum laxet* . . .

Here I cut the verse short, because I had the disconcerting impression—perhaps I was mistaken—that Columba, giving me an almost imperceptible wink, was looking at me with an expression that said: *Quosque tandem, Christoforo?* . . . All the same, making my voice more dramatic, I moved to a higher register: And, through the grace of Your Majesties, I was the one who opened, I was the one who led the way to new horizons, making the world round, like a pear, like the breast of a woman with a nipple in the middle—and my eyes quickly sought those of my Mistress—the world that Pedro Aliaco, the illustrious chancellor of the Sorbonne and Notre Dame de Paris, had seen as *almost* round, *almost* spherical, creating a bridge between Aristotle and me. With me, the prophecy in the Book of Isaiah is fulfilled. Now it has achieved reality: "Their land is filled with silver and gold, and there is no end to their treasures, in a place of broad rivers and streams, where galleys with oar can go, and stately ships can pass."

When I had finished, I knelt down for vespers with a studied expression of nobility, the monarchs knelt down, all those present knelt down, choking back tears, as the six canons and subcanons of the Royal Chapel began the most solemn *Te Deum* ever heard this side of heaven. And when the celestial voices came back to earth, I ordered my seven Indians to begin instruction in Christianity, so that they could be baptized as soon as they had received enough knowledge. "Do not keep them as slaves," said the Queen, "but take them back to their land in the first ship returning there . . ." And that night, I came to see my mistress in the intimacy of her private suite, where I knew the pleasures of seeing her again after a long and difficult absence—and damned if, during those hours, I remembered either caravels or Indians. But a little before sunrise, when we were both lying sated, watching the sky begin to brighten, talking of one thing and another, I thought I noticed that Columba, having had time to reconsider the events of the day and recognize the realities I knew so well, did not seem as completely convinced by my words as I might have wished. I increased my rhetoric, the aptness of my quotations, the skill with which I manipulated images, but she was reserved, reticent, she wouldn't commit herself or express a frank and full opinion about the importance of my enterprise. "So, in a word . . . what do you think of what you saw today?" I asked, to get her started. "What I think is, to bring back seven bleary-eyed little men, sick and sorrowful, a few sticks and leaves that aren't good for anything but fumigating a leper colony, and gold that wouldn't fill a cavity in a molar, it's not worth having spent two million maravedis." "And what about the value to your crowns?" I shouted. "We gained enough prestige with the expulsion of the Jews and the conquest of the kingdom of Granada. Real, lasting prestige comes from things that can be seen and touched, from laws that have repercussions as far away as Rome, from military victories that become part of history . . . But your prestige, if in fact you can earn any, will be in the long term. Up to this point, nothing has happened in these countries, which we can't even imagine, no battles have been won, no memorable triumphs have been achieved—*in hoc signo vinces*—for now, all we have is inspiration that makes blind men cheer and opinions that make your listeners swell up with pleasure, like the heroic feats Charlemagne recounted when he made his victorious entrance to Zaragoza, having humiliated the Babylonian king, when the truth was that, after a siege that was neither glorious nor arduous, he returned to France defeated, leaving a rear guard commanded by Roland the knight, who . . . well! . . . you know what happened . . . " "But I brought back gold!" I insisted: "Everybody saw it. There is a mine there, an enormous mine . . . " "If the mine is so big, your men should have brought back ingots, not the trifles that my jewellers say are not even worth a hundred maravedis." I said it was impossible, in the short time we were *over there*, to undertake the real job of extraction; of the importance of returning as soon as possible to tell of my Discovery. . . . "I had an expert in aromatic plants identify the plants you brought back: he didn't find any cinnamon, or any nutmeg, or pepper, or cloves; therefore, you did not land in the Indies," she said. "Always the imposter." "Then where did I land?" "In a place nothing like any part of the Indies." "And in so doing, I risked my honor and my life." "Not really. Not really. If you hadn't met Master Jacob in Ice Land, you wouldn't have gone off so confidently. You knew that, *no matter what*, come what may, you would arrive at some country." "A country that holds fabulous treasures!" "Apparently not, from what you have shown us." "Then why in the devil did you write to me, ordering me to prepare for a second voyage?" "To screw Portugal," she answered, calmly biting off a piece of Toledan marzipan. "If you don't establish a firm foothold now, the others will get in ahead of us—the ones to whom you almost sold your project, twice, the rulers of Castile and Aragón matter so little to you. They've already sent messengers to the Pope, claiming possession of the lands that your ships barely touched." "So my voyage didn't accomplish anything?" "I wouldn't go that far. But, hell! . . . how complicated life is! Now I have to outfit ships, raise money, postpone the war in Africa, all in order to plant our flag—I have no choice—in countries that, as far as I'm concerned, are neither Ophir, Ophar, nor Cipango. Try to bring back more gold than you brought this time, and pearls, and precious stones, and spices. Then I'll believe in some of these things that still smell to me like more of your tricks."

...When I left the royal bedchamber, I was really stung. I must confess. Some of the things she said made my ears burn. But I was not as upset as I had been before, when no one would finance my proposals. Once again the ocean was in sight. Within a few months, I would again feel the excitement of billowing sails, but with a luff more full and secure than before... And now I would have enough ships; now that scoundrel Martín Alonso was dead; now I would really command my crew, with the title of Admiral, my appointment as Viceroy, and the *Don* in front of my name... I returned to the dockyard where the Indians were shivering under their wool coverlets, and the parrots, having finished vomiting the wine they had gulped down, were lying with their feet in the air, with the glassy eyes of dead fish gone bad, droopy, their feathers ruffled, as if they had been chased by a broom... Soon they would all be dead. As would six of the seven Indians I had exhibited before the throne—some dying of a cough, some of measles, some of diarrhea—a few days after being baptized. From Diegito, the only one left, I knew that these men neither liked nor admired us: they thought we were treacherous, lying, violent, hot-tempered, cruel, dirty, and foul-smelling, since we almost never bathed, unlike them, who freshened their bodies several times a day in the rivers, streams, and waterfalls of their land. They said our houses stank of rancid grease; our narrow streets of shit; our finest horsemen of armpits; and that if our ladies wore so many bodices and ruffles and ribbons, it must be to hide some repulsive deformity or sore—or maybe because they're embarrassed by their breasts, which are so fat that they always seem ready to pop out of their lace tuckers. Our perfumes and scented oils—and even incense—make them sneeze; they choke in our narrow rooms; and they think our churches are places of pain and panic because of the many filthy, crippled, pathetic dwarfs and monsters who clog their entrances. They can't understand why so many men who are not part of an army go about armed, nor how so many richly dressed women on dazzling horses can look down without shame on the perpetual grieving demonstration of misery and purulence, or amputees and beggars in rags. Not only that, but our plan to inculcate in them the doctrines of our religion, before they would receive the lustral waters, had come to nothing. They didn't say that they were unwilling to listen: they said, simply, that they did not understand. If God had created the world and the plants and the animals that populate it, and had pronounced everything in it to be good, they could not see how Adam and Eve, creatures of Divine Creation, could have committed any offense by eating the good fruit from the good tree. They did not think that going perfectly naked was indecent; if the men *over there* wore a loincloth it was because their fragile, sensitive sex, hanging exposed, had to be protected from spiny plants, sharp grasses, and from the attacks, blows, and cuts of predators; as for the women, it was better that they cover their nature with the little pieces of cotton I had seen, so that when the menses was flowing, that distasteful pollution would not be obvious. They did not understand the Old Testament books I showed them either: they could not see why evil was represented by a serpent, since the serpents in their islands were not dangerous. Moreover, the idea of a serpent with an apple in his mouth made them laugh uproariously because—as Diegito explained to me—"snakes don't eat fruit"— . . . Soon we will raise anchor once again and return to the outposts of Cipango that I discovered—although Columba, who was insufferable during this period, perhaps because she needed an outlet for her anxiety, said a hundred times that she had seen no sign of Cipango. And so for the indoctrination of the Indians, she should have employed men more capable than I to perform that mission! Saving souls is not my job. And don't look for the vocation of an apostle in someone who has the gall of a banker. And now what she asked me to do—it was more an order—was to find gold, lots of gold, as much gold as I could, since now—thanks to me—a mirage had been created, a vision of Colchis and the Golden Chersonese.

4

CONQUEST
The Taking of the Americas

We have torn our hair in grief.

AZTEC ELEGY FOR TENOCHTITLÁN

Cruelties of the Spaniards. (1589)

Blackness There Is Indeed

> While I was in the boat, I captured a very beautiful Carib
> woman, whom the aforesaid Lord Admiral gave to me, and
> with whom, having brought her into my cabin, and she being
> naked as is their custom, I conceived the desire to take my
> pleasure. I wanted to put my desire to execution, but she was
> unwilling for me to do so, and treated me with her nails in
> such wise that I would have preferred never to have begun.
> But seeing this (in order to tell you the whole even to the end),
> I took a rope-end and thrashed her well, following which she
> produced such screaming and wailing as would cause you not
> to believe your ears. Finally we reached an agreement such
> that, I can tell you, she seemed to have been raised in a veri-
> table school of harlots.
>
> —MICHELE DE CUNEO, letter to a friend

For the Europeans, America was a whore. They could rape and
then insult her. For all the dreams of paradises and new worlds,
for all the debates about the humanity of the natives, America
was taken by invaders, in a conquest that was partly biological
and partly military warfare. The military campaigns were conducted by competing adventurers, as likely to turn upon each
other as to attack the natives (one thinks, for example, of Balboa,
the discoverer of the Pacific, hanged by his rival Pedrarias).

The newcomers were ruthlessly effective. Kirkpatrick Sale
estimates eight million people were killed on Hispaniola alone.
In *The Conquest of America* Tzvetan Todorov paints an even more
devastating picture: "If the word genocide has ever been applied
to a situation with some accuracy, this is here the case. It consti-
tutes a record not only in relative terms (a destruction on the
order of 90 percent or more), but also in absolute terms, since we
are speaking of a population diminution estimated at 70 million
human lives. None of the great massacres of the twentieth century can be compared to this hecatomb. It will be understood

how vain are the efforts made by certain authors to dissipate what
has been called the 'black legend' of Spain's responsibility for this
genocide. Blackness there is indeed, even if there is no legend."

It is a fascinating campaign, if you can forget the extent of
the destruction it caused. There was heroism and cowardice, resistance and capitulation, self-sacrifice and self-interest on both
sides. The Spanish had inferior numbers and often triumphed
by playing several factions off against each other. Cortés in Mexico, with La Malinche, his native interpreter, was the wiliest of
conquistadores, fighting against the designated representatives
of the crown at the same time he was launching his attack on the
fiercest of American civilizations. In Peru, Pizarro was similarly
victorious against overwhelming odds.

Elsewhere the Spaniards (and the other Europeans who followed) prevailed by ruthless cruelty. In *The Gold of Ophir*, critic
and historian Edward Dahlberg provides a few typical examples:
"Pedro de Alvarado, the lieutenant of Cortés," he begins, "annihilated four to five million natives in the peninsula of Guatemala
and Yucatán within a few years. . . . De Soto lopped off the heads
of Indian couriers because he was too fatigued to remove their
iron collars. Gonzalo Pizarro threw numerous Incas to the dogs,
which devoured them, because they were unable to tell him anything about a land of the cinnamon trees."

Disease may have been the greatest scourge brought from
Europe to America. Nonetheless, the conquest of America was
essentially a military action, probably the deadliest ever; now,
half a millennium after Columbus first touched our lands, we
remember the battles that began the modern history of our
hemisphere.

Thomas Hariot

God Strikes Them Down

Smallpox, measles, and other infectious diseases devastated the native populations of the Americas (in exchange, the Europeans took syphilis home with them). The Europeans seemed to have an unshakable conviction that Providence intended them to take possession of the New World. Religious sentiment could thus be used to justify the unlikeliest atrocities or catastrophes. In this passage, first published in 1588, Thomas Hariot argues that disease was God's means of clearing the way for the colonists.

Thomas Hariot was Walter Raleigh's tutor; Raleigh sent him to join the Virginia colonists after the failure of the first Roanoke colony under Ralph Lane. Hariot proved a bit more resourceful than Lane. He studied native agriculture and identified a variety of native food plants, which he listed in a report on "merchantable commodities." Nonetheless, the English proved incapable of managing these resources, and this colony too failed.

The Europeans failed to master American agricultural skills. According to Carl Sauer in SIXTEENTH CENTURY NORTH AMERICA, *"All European ventures of the century failed with the exception of the cod and whale fisheries, and these had nothing to do with territorial possession by any power."*

The next ship to arrive from England found Hariot's colony mysteriously deserted. More than a century later, travelers heard rumors of white survivors, but no trace of them was ever found.

There was no town where we had any subtile device practiced against us, we leaving it unpunished or not revenged (because we sought by all means possible to win them by gentleness) but that within a few days after our departure from every such town, the people began to die very fast, and many in short space, in some towns about twenty, in some forty, and in one six score, which in truth was very many in respect to their numbers. This happened in no place that we could learn but where we had been where they used such practice against us, and after such time. The disease also was so strange, that they neither knew what it was, nor how to cure it, the like by report of the oldest men in the country never happened before, time out of mind. . . . All the space of their sickness, there was no man of ours known to die, or that was specially sick.

Guillermo Cabrera Infante

So Much Courtesy

Guillermo Cabrera Infante, author of THREE TRAPPED TIGERS *and*
INFANTE'S INFERNO, *published* VIEW OF DAWN IN THE TROPICS, *from
which this excerpt is taken, in* 1974. *This work retells the history of
Cabrera Infante's native Cuba, rather as Eduardo Galeano in his more
sweeping work* MEMORY OF FIRE *retells the history of the hemisphere.*
*   This incident, a massacre in the days of Columbus, sets the tone
for the conquest. It was reported by Bartolomé de Las Casas, who preserved the log of Columbus. A sharp observer, Las Casas is considered
the conscience of the conquest.*

Upon reaching a large village, the conquistadores found some
two thousand Indians gathered in the central square, awaiting
them with gifts—a quantity of fish and also cassava bread—all of
them squatting and some smoking. The Indians began to hand
out the food, when a soldier took out his sword and attacked one
of them, lopping off his head in one stroke. Other soldiers imitated the action of the first and without any provocation began
to swing their swords left and right. There was even greater
butchery when several soldiers entered a *batey*, a very large house
in which over five hundred Indians had gathered, "among
whom few had the chance to escape." Father Las Casas tells us:

"There was a stream of blood as if many cows had been slaughtered." When an investigation of the incident was ordered, it was found out that the conquistadores, receiving such a friendly reception, "thought that so much courtesy was intended to kill them for sure."

Chibcha Tundama

I Reject Peace

In Bogota, Columbia, there is a museum filled with the most magnificent worked-gold artifacts. They are the product of a shadowy civilization called the Chibcha—the kingdom of El Dorado, the Spanish called it—about whom we know much less than we do about the Aztec or the Inca. The Chibcha were traders spanning the region from Mesoamerica to the Incan highlands in the Andes.

Tundama, the defender of Bacata (present-day Bogota) was called upon to surrender to conquistador Baltazar Maldonado in 1541. His is one of the more eloquent voices for resistance. This speech was recorded by yet another conquistador, Jiménez de Quesada, whose manuscript was subsequently lost; this is a portion that was copied and survived.

I am not so barbarous, famous Spaniard, not to believe peace to be the center on which the bounds of this world depend; but do not think I'm unaware that the bland words with which you offer it to me are much belied by your harsh behavior.

Who will say that Tundama should give to the vassal the tribute due to the king? I cannot serve someone who serves his king so badly. According to your own accounts of the King of Spain's clemency, it is not credible that he should send you to kill and rob us so.

More barbarian than the Panches and the Muzos, you bathe your horses's mouth in our blood, which they drink out of hunger and thirst and which you spill to display your cruelty. You desecrate the sanctuaries of our gods and sack the houses of men who haven't offended you. Who would choose to undergo these insults, being not insensitive? Who would omit to rid himself of such harassment, even at the cost of his life?

You well know that my people were bred with no fewer natural privileges than yours. We now know that you are not immortal or descended from the sun. Since your people refuse tax and tyranny you cannot be surprised that mine do, with determination.

Do not take as examples the Zipas, killed sooner through your treachery or their bad government, or because they fought with less right, than because of the valour you claim for yourselves.

Note well the survivors who await you, to undeceive you that victory is always yours.

Chilam Balam

The Battle Flag Is Raised

The richest body of written literature by native peoples from the period of the conquest is that of the Maya who inhabited the Yucatán, southern Mexico, and Central America to Honduras. Once a mighty civilization with its capital in Tikal in the Petén jungle of Guatemala and Belize, the Maya had by the time of the conquest disintegrated into a loose alliance of independent factions with separate dialects and customs. The Spanish won a grudging foothold in the Mayan territories but, as historian Michael D. Coe has written in THE MAYA, *"The Maya are, for all their apparent docility, the toughest Indians of Mesoamerica, and the struggle against European civilization never once halted. . . . The Maya were never completely conquered." Today the population of Guatemala, the heartland of the Maya, is considered more than half pure Mayan and more than 90 percent of part Mayan descent.*

Mayan hieroglyphic writing is found on many stelae and architectural reliefs, much of it reflecting their astronomical expertise, which produced a more accurate calendar than that of the Europeans. (The Mayan calendar was based around eighteen twenty-day months followed by a dread period of five "unlucky days.") The most substantive recordings of Mayan epic and religious literature were made in Spanish in the sixteenth century. Foremost among these are three book-length works: the POPUL VUH, *a Quiche epic poem of great literary merit from highland*

Guatemala that is the most complete account of the cosmogony of Meso-americans and has been called "the Bible of the Americas"; THE ANNALS OF CAKCHIQUEL, also from the highlands; and the CHILAM BALAM, a compilation of community books of the Yucatán Maya.

According to Gordon Brotherston in IMAGE OF THE NEW WORLD, "Chilam Balam or Priest Jaguar, the scholar-sage after whom the Yucatec community books are named, was one of many who anticipated the Spanish invasion of eastern Yucatán from the Caribbean islands. His statements epitomize the energy devoted by the Maya to finding ways of dealing with foreign economies and religions without being destroyed by them." This passage, however, is a song of war that ends with the Mayan warriors scattering into the forests. From there the Maya conducted guerrilla campaigns against the Europeans. In 1847 they nearly regained the Yucatán peninsula; in 1860 they launched another powerful attack. There were major highland Mayan uprisings in 1712 and 1868. In Guatemala and Central America, their struggle continues today.

Eat, eat, you have bread
Drink, drink, you have water
On that day, dust possesses the earth
On that day, a blight is on the face of the earth
On that day, a cloud rises
On that day, a mountain rises
On that day, a strong man seizes the land
On that day, things fall to ruin
On that day, the tender leaf is destroyed
On that day, the dying eyes are closed
On that day, three signs are on the tree
On that day, three generations hang there
On that day, the battle flag is raised
And they are scattered afar in the forests

Miguel Ángel Asturias

Tecúm-Umán

Guatemalan Nobel Prize-winner Miguel Ángel Asturias is the modern writer most directly and consciously influenced by Mayan literature. He studied anthropology and literature in Paris in the twenties, then returned home to write poems, stories, and novels—among them MEN OF MAIZE, LEGENDS OF GUATEMALA, *and* BADTHIEF *(based on the explorations of Balboa)—rooted in the Mayan culture that still thrives, albeit precariously, in Guatemala, the most Indian of all American nations.*

Tecúm-Umán was the Mayan hero who headed up the fight against Pedro de Alvarado ("the Sword of Extremadura"), the leader of a party of Spaniards who traveled south from Mexico to conquer the Maya. (Later de Alvarado tried unsuccessfully to wrest the wealth of the Incas from Pizarro.) Today Tecúm-Umán's feathered image appears throughout Guatemala.

In Asturias's representation, Tecúm-Umán is a warrior-god who embodies the culture of the Maya (who considered themselves "men of maize") and their struggle for survival. Asturias's rhetorical and musical poem emulates the poetry of the POPUL VUH *and the* CHILAM BALAM *at the same time that it evokes the sound of Mayan war drums. His poem is a literary invocation of the spirit of Mayan defiance. Its ending, in which the drums turn to post-conquest bells, suggests that despite the appearance of defeat, the spirit of Tecúm-Umán remains alive, and the battle will continue.*

Tecúm-Umán is clad in quetzal feathers; the long-tailed bird,
which is said to be unable to live in captivity, is a Guatemalan symbol
of freedom. Today it is an endangered species.

Tecúm-Umán, of the green towers,
the green, green towers,
the green, green, green towers
with Indians, Indians, Indians, in Indian file
innumerable as a hundred thousand swarming ants:
ten thousand archers at the foot of the clouds, a thousand
with slings under the poplar trees, seven thousand
blowgunners, and a thousand men wielding axes
atop each butterfly wing
that has dropped into the warriors' anthill.

Tecúm-Umán, of the green plumes,
the long green, green plumes,
the long green, green, green plumes,
green, green, a many-faced quetzal
with moving wings amid the battle,
amid the pommeling of the ears
of the men of maize, scattered
and pecked by birds of fire,
in a net of death, amid the scattered stones.

Quatzalumán, of the green wings
and the long green, green, green tail,
green arrows, green from the green
towers, tattooed with green tattoos.

Tecúm-Umán, of the earth-stampers,
the tributary roaring of the dry

storm of the big brass drums, skins
of calfskin drums, skins
of drums raining skins, skins
inside, skins at the center, skins outside,
skins of drums, drums drums drumming drums
drums drums drumming drums drums drums drumming drums
drums drumming drums, drums drums drumming drums drums
a thunderous medley beat out
with giant seeds in the hollow
of the echo that swells from the timbrels,
timbrels, timbrels, tabor-drums,
tim timbrels tim timbrels
timbrels, timbrels, timbrels . . .

Quetzalumán, of the green cactus-trees,
the green, green cactus-trees,
the green, green, green cactus-trees.
Shafts of the lances with precious
metals in victory of lightning
and torn crests
between the standards of the cactus-trees
and the crumbling of the clouded
earth and the lakes that fill with stones
with the drum of his splashless tumbles.
The drum, Tecúm's weapon of war,
that calls, cries, collects, and produces men
of the earth to wage the dance
of battle, which is the dance of the drum.
The drum, the war drum of Tecúm,
blind within like the tunneled dwelling
of the giant humming-bird, the Quetzal,
the giant humming-bird of Tecúm.

Quetzal, imam of the sun, Tecúm, imam
of the drum, Quetzaltecúm, sun and drum, drum
beat of the lake, drum beat of the mountain, drum
beat of the green, drum beat of the sky, drum,
drum, drum, drum beat of the green heart
of the drum, palpitation of springtime,
in the first springtime drum beat
of the flowers that bathe the living earth.

Grandfather of the left hand and of the right! His great hand
crushes against his chest the Tlascalas
and Spaniards, beasts with human faces!
Lord of Galibal and Master
of quetzals in the testicular
patrimony of the hollow depths, dripping a beard of birds
down to the last generation
of chiefs painted with red annatto
and unruly frijole hair
in tufts of feathers from captive eagles!

Chief of deeds and ramparts
of tribes of fiery stone and clans
of armed volcano! Fire and lava:
Who can explain volcanos without arms?
A race of storms wrapped in plumes
of quetzal, red, green, yellow!
Quetzalumán, the coral serpent
sucks honey of war from the Sequijel,
bleeds the Tree of Prophecy,
the prophecy of raining bloods,
over the hills of quetzals
facing the Sword of Extremadura!

Tecúm-Umán!
Silence in the brush . . .
Mask of pierced night . . .
Tortillas of ashes and dead plumes
under the cover of shadows,
beyond darkness, in darkness, and under darkness without end.
The Sword of Extremadura, with claws
armor, and long lances . . .
Who will the dry eyes call upon?
Whose twisted ears without wind
who will be called . . . who will be called
Tecúm-Umán! Quetzalumán!

His breath is not cut short, for it continues in the calls
A city is armed in his blood
and continues, a fortified city
of bells rather than drums, a mistress
of the seed of winged freedom
green, green, green emerald green
in the giant hummingbird, the quetzal,
a sweet seed that pierces the tongue
which speaks now the word Captain.
Now he is not Tecúm! Now he is not the drum!
Now, he is the tolling of the bells,
Captain.

Bernal Díaz de Castillo

La Malinche

THE DISCOVERY AND CONQUEST OF MEXICO *by Bernal Díaz, an ordinary soldier born the year Columbus first set sail for the Indies, is the
greatest of the contemporaneous chronicles of the conquest. Perhaps not
coincidentally, Díaz was, as critic Julie Greer Johnson has noted in*
WOMEN IN COLONIAL SPANISH AMERICAN LITERATURE, *"the only
early colonial writer to make a woman a major figure in the historical
events unfolding in Spain's American possessions."*

*La Malinche, as she is known—her original name was probably
Malinal; the Spaniards called her Marina—is an archetypal figure
in Mexico, "the Mexican Eve," part of its national mythology and
sense of identity. She is generally a negative figure, for she collaborated
with the Spanish and helped to defeat the Aztecs; moreover, she was
Hernán Cortés's mistress, though he makes little mention of her in his
own writings.*

*Tzvetan Todorov believes that Cortés's triumph in Mexico was a
linguistic triumph, a victory by means of language. For this, La Malinche was invaluable, for she was the most able translator to take part in
the conquest. She was also politically astute, as was Cortés. Notable
among her many contributions were the discovery of an ambush plot at
Cholula and assistance in Cortés's negotiations with Moctezuma.*

After the conquest of Mexico, La Malinche, as has been noted earlier, gave birth to a son by Cortés. Symbolically, this boy, Martín Cortés, was the first mestizo, and Cortés and La Malinche were the symbolic parents of Mexico. In THE LABYRINTH OF SOLITUDE, *Octavio Paz devotes a chapter to "The Sons of La Malinche," in which he argues that for Mexicans La Malinche represents the violated mother. According to this view, her violations and betrayal have left a permanent stain on the Mexicans. They are* hijos de la chingada—*"sons of the bitch."*

The figure of La Malinche appears frequently in Mexican literature. In Carlos Fuentes's ALL CATS ARE GRAY *(the title alludes to the notion that all oppressors are alike) the central character, a resourceful La Malinche, struggles with her position between Moctezuma and Cortés. She also appears in Rosario Castellano's* THE ETERNAL FEMININE, *in Willebaldo López's* MALINCHE SHOW, *and in Sabina Berman's* EAGLE OR SUN. *Sandra Messinger Cypess discusses these and many other treatments of this seminal figure in her useful* LA MALINCHE IN MEXICAN LITERATURE.

In the pantheon of Mexican legend La Malinche's significance is always evolving. Today she seems to be becoming a more sympathetic figure, particularly among Chicana writers: "Any denigrations made against her," Chicana author Adelaida Del Castillo wrote in "Malintzín Tenépal," "indirectly defame the character of the Mexicana/Chicana female. If there is shame for her, there is shame for us; we suffer the effects of these implications."

This selection is Díaz's version of the birth and abandonment of La Malinche and her subsequent reconciliation with her parents. The truthfulness of this story, which has something of the flavor of popular romances of the time, is open to question, but it has become an accepted part of Mexican folklore.

Before telling the story of the great Moctezuma and his famous City of Mexico and the Mexicans, I wish to give an account of Doña Marina, who was born to rule towns and vassals. This is her story.

Doña Marina's father and mother were chiefs and caciques of the town of Paynala and the surrounding towns; Paynala was about eight leagues from the town of Coatzacoalcos. Her father died while she was young and her mother married another cacique, a young man, with whom she had a son. They were very fond of this son and decided that he should inherit their positions after they died. To eliminate any obstacle to this, they gave the little girl, Doña Marina, to some Indians from Xicalango, secretly, by night, so they would not be seen, and then they told everyone that she had died. As it happened, a child of one of their Indian slaves had just died, and they said that it was their daughter, the heiress, who was dead.

The Indians of Xicalango gave the girl to the people of Tabasco and the People of Tabasco gave her to Cortés. I knew Doña Marina's mother when she was an old woman, as well as the old woman's son, Doña Marina's half brother, who grew up to rule the town jointly with his mother after the old woman's second husband had died. After they were baptized as Christians, the old woman was named Marta and the son Lázaro. I know this whole story because in the year 1523, after the conquest of Mexico and other provinces, Cristóbel de Olid revolted in Honduras and Cortés passed through Coatzacoalcos on his way to put down the rebellion, and most of the settlers living in Coatzacoalcos, myself included, joined him and accompanied him on his campaign, which I shall describe in the appropriate time and place. As Doña Marina was such an excellent woman and so useful as an interpreter throughout the wars in New Spain, Tlaxcala, and Mexico (as I shall show later on), Cortés always took her along with him, and during this campaign, she married a man named Juan Jaramillo in the town of Orizaba.

Doña Marina was an extremely important woman and the Indians of New Spain obeyed her unquestioningly.

When Cortés was in Coatzacoalcos, he ordered all the caciques of that province to assemble before him, so that he could preach our holy religion to them and explain why they had been treated so well. Among the assembled caciques was Doña Marina's mother and her half brother, Lázaro.

Some time before this event, Doña Marina had told me that she was from this province and had been born into a ruling family. Cortés and Aguilar, the interpreter, were also aware of this fact. And when mother, daughter, and son were brought together, it was easy to see the strong resemblance Doña Marina bore to her mother.

The mother and son were weeping with fear; they were terrified of Doña Marina, thinking she had sent for them to have them executed.

When Doña Marina saw them in tears, she went over and comforted them, telling them not to be afraid. She said that when they gave her to the Indians from Xicalango, they did not realize what they were doing. She said she forgave them for doing it, and she gave them gold jewels and clothing and sent them away, back to their town. She said that God had been very good to her, freeing her from the worship of idols and converting her to Christianity, allowing her to bear a son for Cortés, her lord and master, and to marry Juan Jaramillo, now her husband. That she would rather serve her husband and Cortés than anything else in the world, and she would not trade places even to be a cacique of all the provinces of New Spain.

Doña Marina knew the language spoken by the people of Coatzacoalcos, which is the same language spoken in Mexico, and she also knew the language of Tabasco. Jerónimo de Aguilar also spoke the language spoken in Tabasco and Yucatán, which is one and the same. So those two spoke to each other, and Aguilar translated into Castillian for Cortés.

And so our new conquests began well, and thanks be to God, we met with great success. I have explained this matter in such detail because without the help of Doña Marina, we would have understood nothing of the language of New Spain and Mexico.

Hernán Cortés

Massacre at Cholula

Hernán Cortés's own account of the Mexican campaign, recorded in his letters—the CARTAS DE RELACIÓN *("Report of Events")—to Emperor Charles V, is one of the clearest and most informative. This passage describes his preemptive massacre of the Cholulans after he had learned from La Malinche of their plans for ambush. Cortés downplays her contribution, a marked contrast with other accounts. This incident is the basis for the opening of Carlos Fuentes's novel* A CHANGE OF SKIN, *in which Cortés puts the torch to the towers and fortresses of Cholula, and "upon the ruins of Cholula are built four hundred churches, their foundations the razed cues, the platforms of the pyramids."*

The people of Tascalteca said that I should not leave Tascalteca until the chiefs of Cholula had come. I spoke to the Cholulan messengers and told them that their chiefs should present themselves before me within three days to swear obedience to Your Highness and offer themselves as your vassals. . . . The next day, many of the chiefs of Cholula appeared before me, saying that if they had not come previously it was because the Tascaltecans were their enemies and they did not wish to enter their land because they felt unsafe there. They said that I had probably heard unfavorable things about them, which I should not believe, because they were the lies of their enemies, not the truth; that I should go to their city and there I would see that what I had been told by the Tascaltecans was all false and what the chiefs were telling me was all true. They offered to serve as vassals to Your Holy Majesty from then on; they swore eternal allegiance and obedience in all things that Your Holy Majesty commanded them. With the assistance of my translators, a notary prepared a document attesting to all of this. Still I was resolved to travel with them to Cholula; on the one hand, to demonstrate my strength, and on the other, because I wanted to conduct my business with Moctezuma from that city, since it bordered on his territory, as I have said, and there is free movement between the two provinces, with an open road and an unrestricted border.

When the Tascaltecans found out what I planned to do, they were very distressed; they told me again and again that I was making a mistake; since they were Your Holy Majesty's vassals, as well as my friends, they wanted to go with me to help me in whatever might happen. Although I was opposed to this plan and told them it was unnecessary to come, some hundred thousand men—all armed for war—followed me to within two leagues of Cholula. It took considerable persuasion on my part to convince them to turn back, and even then about five or six thousand remained with me. That night I slept in a ditch, hoping to distance myself from these followers in case they started trouble in the city; it was already late and I did not wish to enter Cholula so late. The next morning, the Cholulans came from their city to greet me, playing trumpets and drums. Among them were many priests from their temples, dressed in their traditional priestly robes and singing in their traditional style, as they do in the temples. They escorted us into the city with a great deal of ceremony and led us to excellent quarters, where everyone in my company was quite comfortable. While there we received information about conditions in the city: the high road had been closed and another road built; there were some holes, although not too many; several city streets had been barricaded; and there were stones on all the rooftops. The natives of Tascalteca had warned us about many of these signs. We became increasingly alert and cautious.

Several of Moctezuma's messengers were in Cholula and they came and spoke with some of my companions, but all they told me was that they had come to find out from the men around me what our plans were, so that they could return to their master and tell him. After they had spoken with my companions, the messengers left, taking with them one of the most important of the men who had been with me before. We stayed in Cholula three days, and each day they fed us worse. Very few Cholulan lords and dignitaries came to visit me and speak with me. I found this quite disturbing. My translator, who is an Indian woman from Putunchan, which is the great river that I described to Your Majesty in my first letter, was told by another Indian woman, a native of Cholula, that many of Moctezuma's men were camped nearby, and that the men of Cholula had sent away their women and children and moved all their belongings outside the city, and that they were about to fall upon us and massacre us; the native woman told my translator that if she wished to escape, she should go with the native, who would hide her. My Indian translator told all this to Gerónimo de Aguilar—Your Highness is already acquainted with this name and I also have written of this translator, whom I acquired in Yucatán, in an earlier letter—and he told me. Because of this news, and some signs we had seen, I moved quickly to forestall an attack: I sent for some of the city chiefs, saying that I wished to speak with them. I shut them in a room, having already advised my men to listen for my signal and, when they heard the sound of a harquebus being fired, to attack the huge group of Indians outside our quarters as well as the chiefs who were inside. And this is what we did: I left the chiefs tied up in an interior room and rode off and ordered the harquebus to be fired, and the battle began; we fought so hard that more than three thousand men were killed in two hours. Your Majesty should know that the Cholulans were thoroughly prepared for this fight: even before I left my quarters every street was filled with their people, all of whom were ready to attack; but we took them by surprise, so they were easy to disperse, especially since they were without leaders. Still, they attacked us from several towers and fortified houses, and I ordered these to be put to the torch. Our quarters were in a strong position and so remained secure while my men and I, plus some five thousand Indians from Tascalteca and another four hundred from Cempoal, ranged through the streets of Cholula, in a battle that lasted five hours or more. Finally, every Cholulan warrior had been driven from the city and scattered to the four winds.

William H. Prescott

A Stain, Never to Be Effaced

One of the most infamous incidents in the conquest of the Americas was Pizarro's assassination of Atahuallpa, "the last of the Incas."

In Peru, as in Mexico, the conquerors were able to take advantage of existing struggles for power. At its peak, the Incan empire included the greater part of western South America, extending from Ecuador to Chile. But in 1525, on the death of the Inca Huayna Capac, the empire was divided. Atahuallpa ruled the northern half of the empire from Quito, Ecuador; his half brother, Huascar, ruled the south from Cuzco, Peru. Atahuallpa had defeated Huascar in civil war just prior to the arrival of Pizarro.

Pizarro invited Atahuallpa to a peace parlay, then seized and imprisoned him. He demanded the fabulous ransom of a room filled with gold and silver. This, incredibly, the Incas delivered. Still Atahuallpa was not released. Instead, he was brought to trial on charges of murder, sedition, and idolatry, and condemned to death by fire, over the protest of Pizarro's most influential advisors.

William H. Prescott, the great American historian, was a fine storyteller. His strength lay less in interpretation and analysis than in the arrangement of materials in a coherent and continuous story. But his passionate involvement in this tale gives his work an emotional commitment that only the best histories achieve. Although some of his sources have proved unreliable, his books, written in the nineteenth century, remain stylish introductions to the events of the conquest.

Pizarro's contemporaries judged him harshly. In Prescott's opinion, they were justified.

The treatment of Atahuallpa, from first to last, forms undoubtedly one of the darkest chapters in Spanish colonial history. There may have been massacres perpetrated on a more extended scale, and executions accompanied with a greater refinement of cruelty. But the blood-stained annals of the Conquest afford no such example of cold-hearted and systematic persecution, not of an enemy, but of one whose whole deportment had been that of a friend and a benefactor.

From the hour that Pizarro and his followers had entered within the sphere of Atahuallpa's influence, the hand of friendship had been extended to them by the natives. Their first act, on crossing the mountains, was to kidnap the monarch and massacre his people. The seizure of his person might be vindicated, by those who considered the end as justifying the means, on the ground that it was indispensable to secure the triumphs of the Cross. But no such apology can be urged for the massacre of the unarmed and helpless population,—as wanton as it was wicked.

The long confinement of the Inca had been used by the Conquerors to wring from him his treasures with the hard grip of avarice. During the whole of this dismal period, he had conducted himself with singular generosity and good faith. He had opened a free passage to the Spaniards through every part of his empire; and had furnished every facility for the execution of their plans. When these were accomplished, he remained an encumbrance on their hands, notwithstanding their engagement, expressed or implied, to release him,—and Pizarro, as we have seen, by a formal act, acquitted his captive of any further obligation on the score of ransom,—he was arraigned before a mock tribunal, and, under pretences equally false and frivolous, was condemned to an excruciating death. From first to last, the policy of the Spanish conquerors towards their unhappy victim is stamped with barbarity and fraud.

It is not easy to acquit Pizarro of being in a great degree responsible for this policy. His partisans have labored to show, that it was forced on him by the necessity of the case, and that in the death of the Inca, especially, he yielded reluctantly to the importunities of others. But weak as is this apology, the historian who has the means of comparing the various testimony of the period will come to a different conclusion. To him it will appear, that Pizarro had probably long felt the removal of Atahuallpa as essential to the success of his enterprise. He foresaw the odium that would be incurred by the death of his royal captive without sufficient grounds; while he labored to establish these, he still shrunk from the responsibility of the deed, and preferred to perpetrate it in obedience to the suggestions of others, rather than his own. Like many an unprincipled politician, he wished to reap the benefit of a bad act and let others take the blame of it.

Almagro and his followers are reported by Pizarro's secretaries to have first insisted on the Inca's death. They were loudly supported by the treasurer and royal officers, who considered it as indispensable to the interests of the Cross; and, finally, the rumors of a conspiracy raised the same cry among the soldiers, and Pizarro, with all his tenderness for his prisoner, could not refuse to bring him to trial.—The form of a trial was necessary to give an appearance of fairness to the proceedings. That it was only form is evident from the indecent haste with which it was conducted,—the examination of evidence, the sentence, and the execution, being all on the same day. The multiplication of the charges, designed to place the guilt of the accused on the strongest ground, had, from their very number, the opposite effect, proving only the determination to convict him. If Pizarro had felt the reluctance to his conviction which he pretended, why did he send De Soto, Atahuallpa's best friend, away, when the inquiry was to be instituted? Why was the sentence so summarily executed, as not to afford opportunity, by that cavalier's return, of disproving the truth of the principal charge,—the only one, in fact, with which the Spaniards had any concern? The solemn farce of mourning and deep sorrow affected by Pizarro, who by these honors to the dead would intimate the sincere regard he had entertained for the living, was too thin a veil to impose on the most credulous.

It is not intended by these reflections to exculpate the rest of the army, and especially its officers, from their share in the infamy of the transaction. But Pizarro, as commander of the army, was mainly responsible for its measures. For he was not a man to allow his own authority to be wrested from his grasp, or to yield timidly to the impulses of others. He did not even yield to his own. His whole career shows him, whether for good or for evil, to have acted with a cool and calculating policy.

A story has been often repeated, which refers to the motives of Pizarro's conduct, in some degree at least, to personal resentment. The Inca had requested one of the Spanish soldiers to write the name of God on his nail. This the monarch showed to several of his guards successively, and, as they read it, and each pronounced the same word, the sagacious mind of the barbarian was delighted with what seemed to him little short of a miracle, —to which the science of his own nation afforded no analogy. On showing the writing to Pizarro, that chief remained silent; and the Inca, finding he could not read, conceived a contempt for the commander who was even less informed than his soldiers. This he did not wholly conceal, and Pizarro, aware of the cause of it, neither forgot nor forgave it. The anecdote is reported not on the highest authority. It may be true; but it is unnecessary to look for the motives of Pizarro's conduct in personal pique, when so many proofs are to be discerned of a dark and deliberate policy.

Yet the arts of the Spanish chieftain failed to reconcile his countrymen to the atrocity of his proceedings. It is singular to observe the difference between the tone assumed by the first chroniclers of the transaction, while it was yet fresh, and that of those who wrote when the lapse of a few years had shown the tendency of public opinion. The first boldly avow the deed as demanded by expediency, if not necessity; while they deal in no measured terms of reproach with the character of their unfortunate victim.

The latter, on the other hand, while they extenuate the errors of the Inca, and do justice to his good faith, are unreserved in their condemnation of the Conquerors, on whose conduct, they say, Heaven set the seal of its own reprobation, by bringing them all to an untimely and miserable end. The sentence of contemporaries has been fully ratified by that of posterity, and the persecution of Atahuallpa is regarded with justice as having left a stain, never to be effaced, on the Spanish arms in the New World.

Tzvetan Todorov

The Conquest of America

Mighty bloody struggles and continuous warfare marked the first cen-
tury of post-Columbian America. It was a battlefield. These hostilities
are not forgotten.

    What was won and what was lost? In this excerpt from THE CON-
QUEST OF AMERICA, *Tzvetan Todorov considers Las Casas's prophecy*
that God would "vent upon Spain His wrath and His fury" for the out-
rages of the conquest.

    According to Todorov, the violence of the conquest reflected an in-
ability to comprehend the Other and "experience difference in equality."
By denying the difference of the external Other, Western civilization
created an internal Other, and there was hell in paradise.

    As we have noted, Todorov believes that "this period of European
history is, in its turn, coming to an end today." By respecting otherness,
we can achieve a multicultural society. The colonized too reject this
Western notion of the Other, calling for a distinction between "an
alienating nothing of Otherness" and "an empowering notion of differ-
ence," in the words of Trinh Minh-ha, author of WOMAN, NATIVE,
OTHER: WRITING POSTCOLONIALITY AND FEMINISM.

At the very end of his life, Las Casas writes in his will: "I believe
that because of these impious, criminal and ignominious deeds

perpetrated so unjustly, tyrannically and barbarously, God will vent upon Spain His wrath and His fury, for nearly all of Spain has shared in the bloody wealth usurped at the cost of so much ruin and slaughter."

These words, half prophecy and half curse, establish the collective responsibility of the Spaniards—and not merely of the conquistadors—for all time to come and not merely the present. And they announce that the crime will be punished, that the sin will be expiated.

We are in a good position today to decide if Las Casas saw matters clearly or not. We can make a slight correction to the extent of his prophecy and replace Spain by "Western Europe": even if Spain takes the lead in the movement of colonization and destruction of the other, Spain is not alone: Portugal, France, England, Holland will follow close after, Belgium, Italy, and Germany will try to catch up. And if in matters of destruction the Spaniards do more than the other European nations, it is not because the latter have not tried to equal and to exceed them. Let us read, then: "God will vent upon Europe His wrath and His fury," if that can make us feel more directly concerned.

Has the prophecy come true? Each of us will answer this question according to his own judgment. For myself, conscious though I am of how arbitrary any estimation of the present is likely to be when the collective memory has not yet performed its sifting function, and hence of the ideological choice implied here, I prefer to assume my vision of events openly, without disguising it as a description of events themselves. Doing so, I choose in the present circumstances the elements that seem to me the most characteristic, that consequently contain—or should contain—the future in germ. Inevitably, these remarks will remain quite elliptical.

Certainly many events of recent history seem to bear Las Casas out. Slavery has been abolished for a hundred years, and the old-style (à l'espagnole) colonialism for about twenty. Many acts of revenge have been and are still taken against citizens of the former colonial powers, whose sole personal crime is that of belonging to the nation in question; the English, the Americans, the French are thus often held to be collectively responsible for their former colonized peoples. I do not know if we are to regard this as the effect of divine wrath and fury, but I think that two reactions are inevitable for anyone familiar with the exemplary history of the conquest of America: first of all, that such retaliatory actions never succeed in righting the balance of the crimes perpetrated by the Europeans (and because of that, such actions can be absolved); next, that such actions merely reproduce the worst of what the Europeans have already accomplished, and nothing is more distressing than to see history repeating itself— even when it is a matter of the history of destruction. That Europe should in her turn be colonized by the peoples of Africa, of Asia, or of Latin America (we are far from this, I know) would perhaps be a "sweet revenge," but cannot be considered my ideal.

A Mayan woman died, devoured by dogs. Her story, reduced to a few lines, concentrates one of the extreme versions of the relation to the other. Her husband, of whom she is the "internal other," already leaves her no possibility of asserting herself as a free subject: fearing to be killed in war, he seeks to ward off the danger by depriving the woman of her will; but war will not be only an affair among men: even when her husband is dead, the wife must continue to belong to him. When the Spanish conquistador appears, this woman is no more than the site where the desires and wills of two people meet. To kill men, to rape women: these are at once proof that a man wields power and his reward. The wife chooses to obey her husband and the rules of her own society; she puts all that remains of her personal will into defending the violence of which she has been the object. But, in fact, a cultural exteriority will determine the outcome of this little drama: she is not raped, as a Spanish woman might have been in time of war; she is thrown to the dogs because she is both an unconsenting woman and an Indian woman. Never was the fate of the other more tragic.

I am writing this book to prevent this story and a thousand others like it from being forgotten. I believe in the necessity of "seeking the truth" and in the obligation of making it known; I know that the function of information exists, and that the effect of information can be powerful. My hope is not that Mayan women will now have European men thrown to the dogs (an absurd supposition, obviously), but that we remember what can happen if we do not succeed in discovering the other.

For the other remains to be discovered. The fact is worthy of astonishment, for man is never alone, and would not be what he is without his social dimension. And yet this is the call: for the newborn child, *his* world is *the* world, and growth is an apprenticeship in exteriority and sociality; we might say, somewhat cavalierly, that human life is confined between these two extremes, one where the *I* invades the world, and one where the world ultimately absorbs the *I* in the form of a corpse or of ashes. And just as the discovery of the other knows several degrees, from the other-as-object, identified with the surrounding world, to the other-as-subject, equal to the *I* but different from it, with an infinity of intermediary nuances, we can indeed live our lives without ever achieving a full discovery of the other (supposing that such a discovery can be made). Each of us must begin it over again in turn; the previous experiments do not relieve us of our responsibility, but they can teach us the effects of misreading the facts.

Yet even if the discovery of the other must be assumed by each individual and eternally recommenced, it also has a history, forms that are socially and culturally determined. The history of the conquest of America makes me believe that a great change occurred—or, rather, was revealed—at the dawn of the sixteenth century, say between Columbus and Cortés; a similar difference (not similar in details, of course) can be observed between Moctezuma and Cortés; this difference functions, then, in time as in space, and if I have lingered over the spatial contrast more than the temporal one, it is because the latter is blurred by countless transitions whereas the former, with the help of an ocean, has all the necessary distinctness. Since the period of the conquest, for almost three hundred and fifty years, Western Europe has tried to assimilate the other, to do away with an exterior alterity, and has in great part succeeded. Its way of life and its values have spread around the world; as Columbus wished, the colonized peoples have adopted our customs and have put on clothes.

This extraordinary success is chiefly due to one specific feature of Western civilization which for a long time was regarded as a feature of man himself, its development and prosperity among Europeans thereby becoming proof of their natural superiority: it is, paradoxically, Europeans' capacity to understand the other. Cortés affords us a splendid example of this, and he was conscious of the degree to which the art of adaptation and of improvisation governed his behavior. Schematically this behavior is organized into two phases. The first is that of interest in the other, at the cost of a certain empathy or temporary identification. Cortés slips into the other's skin, but in a metaphoric and no longer a literal fashion: the difference is considerable. Thereby he ensures himself an understanding of the other's language and a knowledge of the other's political organization (whence his interest in the Aztecs' internal dissension, and he even masters the emission of messages in an appropriate code: hence he manages to pass himself off as Quetzalcóatl returned to earth. But in so doing he has never abandoned his feeling of superiority; it is even his very capacity to understand the other that confirms him in that feeling. Then comes the second phase, during which he is not content to reassert his own identity (which he has never really abandoned), but proceeds to assimilate the Indians to his own world. In the same way, it will be recalled, the Franciscan monks adopted the Indians' ways (clothes, food) to convert them more effectively to the Christian religion. The Europeans exhibit remarkable qualities of flexibility and improvisation which permit them all the better to impose their own way of life. Of course, this capacity of simultaneous adaptation and absorption is not at all a universal value and with it brings its converse, which is much less appreciated. Egalitarianism, of which one version is characteristic of the (Western) Christian religion as well as of the ideology of modern capitalistic states, also serves colonial expansion: here is another, somewhat surprising lesson of our exemplary history.

At the same time that it was tending to obliterate the strangeness of the external other, Western civilization found an interior other. From the classical age to the end of romanticism (i.e., down to our day), writers and moralists have continued to discover that the person is not *one*—or is even nothing—that *Je est un autre*, or a simple echo chamber, a hall of mirrors. We no longer believe in wild men in the forests, but we have discovered the beast in man, "that mysterious thing in the soul, which seems to acknowledge no human jurisdiction, but in spite of the individual's own innocent self, will still dream horrid dreams, and mutter unmentionable thoughts" (Melville, *Pierre*, IV,2). The instauration of the unconscious can be considered as the culminating point of this discovery of the other in oneself.

I believe that this period of European history is, in its turn, coming to an end today. The representatives of Western civilization no longer believe so naively in its superiority, and the movement of assimilation is running down in that quarter, even if the recent or ancient nations of the Third World still want to live like the Europeans. On the ideological level, at least, we are trying to combine what we regard as the better parts of both terms of the alternative; we want *equality* without its compelling us to accept identity; but also *difference* without its degenerating into the superiority / inferiority. We aspire to reap the benefits of the egalitarian model *and* of the hierarchic mode; we aspire to rediscover the meaning of the social without losing the quality of the individual. The Russian socialist Alexander Herzen wrote in the middle of the nineteenth century: "To understand the extent, reality, and sacred nature of the rights of the person without destroying society, without fracturing it into atoms: such is the most difficult social goal." We are still telling ourselves the same thing today.

To experience difference in equality is easier said than done. Yet several figures of my exemplary history came close to it, in various ways. On the axiological level, a Las Casas managed in his old age to love and esteem the Indians as a function not of his own ideal, but of theirs: this is a nonunifying love, one

might even say a "neutral" one, to use the word as Blanchot and
Barthes do. On the level of action, of the assimilation of the
other or of identification with him, a Cabeza de Vaca also reached
a neutral point, not because he was indifferent to the two cultures but because he had experienced them both from within—
thereby, he no longer had anything but "the others" around
him; without becoming an Indian, Cabeza de Vaca was no longer
quite a Spaniard. His experience symbolizes and heralds that of
the modern exile, which in its turn personifies a tendency characteristic of our society: a being who has lost his country without thereby acquiring another, who lives in a double exteriority.
It is the exiled person who today best incarnates, though warp-
ing it from its original meaning, the ideal of Hugh of St. Victor,
who formulated it this way in the twelfth century: "The man
who finds his country sweet is only a raw beginner; the man for
whom each country is as his own is already strong; but only the
man for whom the whole world is as a foreign country is perfect." (I myself, a Bulgarian living in France, borrow this quotation from Edward Said, a Palestinian living in the United
States, who himself found it in Erich Auerbach, a German exiled
in Turkey.)

Finally, on the level of knowledge, a Durán and a Sahagún
heralded, without fully achieving, the dialogue of cultures that
characterizes our age and which is incarnated by ethnology, at
once the child of colonialism and the proof of its death throes: a
dialogue in which no one has the last word, in which neither
voice is reduced to the status of a simple object, and in which we
gain advantage from our externality to the other. Durán and
Sahagún are ambiguous symbols, for theirs are medieval minds;
perhaps it is this very exteriority to the culture of their time that
is responsible for their modernity. Through these different examples one characteristic is asserted: a new exotopy (to speak in
Bakhtine's fashion), an affirmation of the other's exteriority which
goes hand in hand with the recognition of the other as subject.
Here perhaps is not only a new way of experiencing alterity, but
also a characteristic feature of our time, as individualism (or

autotelism) was for the period whose end we are now beginning to discern.

That is what an optimist like Levinas would propose: "Our period is not defined by the triumph of technology for technology's sake, as it is not defined by art for art's sake, as it is not defined by nihilism. It is action for a world to come, transcendence of its period—transcendence of self which calls for epiphany of Other."

Walt Whitman

Prayer of Columbus

With his vision of paradise and his creation of hell, Columbus has exerted a powerful hold on the North American imagination, particularly since the Columbus boom in the nineteenth century.

Washington Irving noted Martín Fernández de Navarrete's discovery of Las Casas's copy of the log of Columbus and other Columbus documents, and he shared the new information about the discoverer in his four-volume LIFE AND VOYAGES OF COLUMBUS, published in 1828. According to Kirkpatrick Sale, between then and the quatercentennial celebration in 1892 "more than several hundred" poems about Columbus were written in English, including efforts by James Russell Lowell, Ralph Waldo Emerson, Edward Everett Hale, Joaquin Miller, and Alfred Tennyson, to name but a few. This flurry of Columbiana led to the extravaganza of the quatercentenary, when enthusiasm for Columbus reached its all-time peak.

Walt Whitman, with his love of national themes, could hardly ignore Columbus. In his "Prayer of Columbus," Whitman portrays the sanctimonious Columbus as a religious visionary; he ignores completely Columbus's role as conqueror. The poem celebrates the "batter'd, wreck'd old man" who had rebounded to such astonishing popularity. For Whitman, it is Columbus's religious conviction that enables him to triumph over adversity through truth.

A batter'd, wreck'd old man,
Thrown on this savage shore, far, far from home,
Pent by the sea and dark rebellious brows, twelve dreary months,
Sore, stiff with many toils, sicken'd and nigh to death,
I take my way along the island's edge,
Venting a heavy heart.

I am too full of woe!
Haply I may not live another day;
I cannot rest O God, I cannot eat or drink or sleep,
Till I put forth myself, my prayer, once more to Thee,
Breathe, bathe myself once more in Thee, commune with Thee,
Report myself once more to Thee.

Thou knowest my years entire, my life,
My long and crowded life of active work, not adoration merely;
Thou knowest the prayers and vigils of my youth,
Thou knowest my manhood's solemn and visionary meditations,
Though knowest how before I commenced I devoted all to come to Thee,
Thou knowest I have in age ratified all those vows and strictly kept them,
Thou knowest I have not once lost nor faith nor ecstasy in Thee,
In shackles, prison'd, in disgrace, repining not,
Accepting all from Thee, as duly come from Thee.

All my emprises have been fill'd with Thee,
My speculations, plans, begun and carried on in thoughts of Thee,
Sailing the deep or journeying the land for Thee;
Intentions, purports, aspirations mine, leaving results to Thee.

O I am sure they really came from Thee,
The urge, the ardor, the unconquerable will,

The potent, felt interior command, stronger than words,
A message from the Heavens whispering to me even in sleep,
These sped me on.

By me and these the work so far accomplish'd,
By me earth's elder cloy'd and stifled lands uncloy'd, unloos'd,
By me the hemispheres rounded and tied, the unknown to the known.

The end I know not, it is all in Thee,
Or small or great I know not—haply what broad fields, what lands,
Haply the brutish measureless human undergrowth I know,
Transplanted there may rise to stature, knowledge worthy Thee,
Haply the swords I know may there indeed be turn'd to reaping-tools,
Haply the lifeless cross I know, Europe's dead cross, may bud and
      blossom there.

One effort more, my altar this bleak sand;
That Thou O God my life hast lighted,
With ray of light, steady, ineffable, vouchsafed of Thee,
Light rare untellable, lighting the very light,
Beyond all signs, descriptions, languages;
For that O god, be it my latest word, here on my knees,
Old, poor, and paralyzed, I thank Thee.

My terminus near,
The clouds already closing in upon me,
The voyage balk'd, the course disputed, lost,
I yield my ships to Thee.

My hands, my limbs grow nerveless,
My brain feels rack'd, bewilder'd,

Let the old timbers part, I will not part,
I will cling fast to Thee, O God, though the waves buffet me,
Thee, Thee at least I know.

Is it the prophet's thought I speak, or am I raving?
What do I know of life? what of myself?
I know not even my own work past or present,
Dim ever-shifting guesses of it spread before me,
Of newer better worlds, their mighty parturition,
Mocking, perplexing me.

And these things I see suddenly, what mean they?
As if some miracle, some hand divine unseal'd my eyes,
Shadowy vast shapes smile through the air and sky,
And on the distant waves sail countless ships,
And anthems in new tongues I hear saluting me.

Jimmie Durham

Columbus Day

*In "Columbus Day," Jimmie Durham, poet and Wolf Clan Cherokee,
sees Columbus at the head of a "bloodline" of "filthy murderers." He suggests reclaiming America from the conquest, from the schoolbook story
of "heroic discoveries made by liars and crooks." The Europeans, as
Carlos Fuentes says, took possession of the land by a process of naming;
Jimmie Durham wants to repossess it today in the same way, by "saying
the right things in the right way," by naming "a few of the victims,"
and naming "our grandchildren . . . in their honor, and bearing the
land itself sing those names."*

In school I was taught the names
Columbus, Cortéz, and Pizarro and
A dozen other filthy murderers.
A bloodline all the way to General Miles,
Daniel Boone and General Eisenhower.

No one mentioned the names
Of even a few of the victims.
But don't you remember Chaske, whose spine
was crushed so quickly by Mr. Pizarro's boot?
What words did he cry into the dust?

What was the familiar name
Of that young girl who danced so gracefully
That everyone in the village sang with her—
Before Cortéz' sword hacked off her arms
As she protested the burning of her sweetheart?

That young man's name was Many Deeds,
And he had been a leader of a band of fighters
Called the Redstick Hummingbirds, who slowed
The March of Cortéz' army with only a few
Spears and stones which now lay still
In the mountains and remember.

Greenrock Woman was the name
Of that old lady who walked right up
And spat in Columbus's face. We
Must remember that, and remember
Laughing Otter the Taino, who tried to stop
Columbus and who was taken away as a slave.
We never saw him again.

In school I learned of heroic discoveries
Made by liars and crooks. The courage
Of millions of sweet and true people
Was not commemorated.

Let us then declare a holiday
For ourselves, and make a parade that begins
With Columbus' victims and continues
Even to our grandchildren who will be named
In their honor.
Because isn't it true that even the summer
Grass here in this land whispers those names,
And every creek has accepted the responsibility
Of singing those names? And nothing can stop
The wind from howling those names around
The corners of the school.

Why else would the birds sing
So much sweeter here than in other lands?

Indians Mining Silver, an illustration by Thèodor de Bry for Bartolomé de Las Casas's *The Destruction of the Indies* (1552).

5
MINING EDEN
Procuring Souls & Precious Metals

It was the Crown of Thorns.

> **MICHAEL DORRIS & LOUISE ERDRICH,**
> *The Crown of Columbus*

A Slave Economy

Gold is most excellent,
gold is a treasure!
With gold you can do
whatever you like in
this world,
even send souls
to Paradise.

—CHRISTOPHER COLUMBUS

In Columbus's journals his greed approaches a frenzy. His long-
ing for gold takes on the character of an aching refrain in a song
of desire for greater and greater riches.

Still, Tzvetan Todorov is able to see Columbus as a religious
man who was driven to this obsession with gold by the demands
of his royal patrons, the king and queen who considered Columbus's discovery to be of little importance when compared to the
recent triumphs of Spanish Christianity in the form of the expulsion of the Jews and Moors. In *The Conquest of America* Todorov
writes that "greed is not Columbus's true motive: if wealth matters to him, it is because wealth signifies the acknowledgment of
his role as discoverer; but he himself would prefer the rough garment of a monk. . . . The universal victory of Christianity—this
is the motive that animates Columbus . . ." For the Europeans,
God was another weapon in the conquest of America.

While the monks who followed Columbus to America saw
the Indians as souls to be gathered for Jesus as well as laborers
on their missions, Columbus saw the Indians as America's main
resource. In Bartolomé de Las Casas's memorable phrase, the
American people were regarded as timber to be felled and trans-
ported at the whim of the conquerors. Columbus was first; he

established the slave economy of the Americas over the opposition of the Spanish church and state. But Columbus was as great a failure as a slaver as he was as a governor. The Indian slaves were used so harshly that they perished. Black slaves were imported, and within thirty years of Columbus's voyage of discovery, the first revolt of the blacks and the few surviving Indians, workers in the mills of Hispaniola, had already been brutally crushed. In the words of Eduardo Galeano, the rebels hung "from gallows scattered along the highways."

The Indians served the European lust for gold in other ways. Columbus set the Taino Indians on Hispaniola to mining to provide the gold he demanded as tribute, and he instituted harsh punishments for failure to provide that tribute. Cortés and Pizarro consigned vast numbers of Indians to mining, particularly in Mexico, Peru, Bolivia, and Chile, where their descendants work the mines to this day. (In our century, the Andean Indian mineworkers' cause was championed with particular eloquence by Peruvian poet César Vallejo.)

The Franciscan Toribio Benavente, called Fray Motolinia, "the poor one," by the Indians, was among the first of the friars to describe the mines of Mexico. In his book *The Gold of Ophir,* Edward Dahlberg summarized his account: "Fray Motolinia, a mild and good man," Dahlberg writes, "blamed the Spaniards for the ten plagues in Mexico. The worst, the monk said, were the gold mines where the Aztecan laborer had to toil until he perished. He was compelled to furnish all the materials for the mines and even his own food. Often he ran for thirty leagues with the little maize he had and died on the way. For half a league from Oaxaca, the principal mining town, the ground was so bleached with human bones that one could not go in that direction without stepping upon skeletons."

America itself was seen as a resource to be mined and removed to private coffers in the homeland. European conquerors regarded the natural resources of land, water, and living beings as temporary assets—private and expendable property rather than a collective resource.

"If we ask ourselves what has heightened our sense of loss in North America, what has made us feel around in the dark for a place where we might take a stand," writes naturalist and author Barry Lopez, "we would have to answer that it is the particulars of what is now called the environmental crisis. Acid rain. Soil erosion. Times Beach. Falling populations of wild animals. But what we really face, I think, is something much larger, something that goes back to Guanahaní [site of Columbus's first landfall] and what Columbus decided to do, that series of acts—theft, rape, and murder—of which the environmental crisis is symptomatic. What we face is a crisis of culture, a crisis of character. Five hundred years after the *Niña*, the *Pinta*, and the *Santa María* sailed into the Bahamas, we are asking ourselves what has been the price of the assumptions those ships carried, particularly about the primacy of material wealth."

Were the Europeans worse than other civilizations? According to Kirkpatrick Sale in *The Conquest of Paradise*, "Nowhere else was the essential reverence for nature seriously challenged, nowhere did there emerge the idea that human achievement and material betterment were to be won by *opposing* nature, nowhere any equivalent to that frenzy of defiance and destruction that we find on the Western record." However we judge their relative guilt, they did lay waste to the garden that had been America.

Alejo Carpentier

Columbus Contemplates Slavery

In this selection from THE HARP AND THE SHADOW, *Columbus, on his deathbed awaiting the confessor who will perform the last rites, recalls the temptation that led him to slave trading. After his first mad search for the gold that will make his voyages profitable, he begins to suspect that the great mine he is seeking may not be forthcoming. Now gold becomes symbolic: it represents vast treasures, which Columbus cannot actually produce. But America must yield some actual wealth. Thus, in his description, its people, whom he once considered the finest in the world, are transformed into cannibals so that they can become his greatest resource.*

The Indian slave trade was ended by the crown, which had more doubts than Columbus seemed to have about its moral and legal validity, and Columbus was made to return some of the spoils of his slaving (nonetheless, he died a rich man—although a bitter one who felt he deserved more). In the nineteenth century, when Rome debated the proposal to canonize Columbus, his involvement in the slave trade was one of the most damning charges against him.

Islands, islands, islands . . . A large one, a tiny one, a harsh one, a mild one; a bald island, a hairy island, an island with gray sand and dead lichens; an island with pebbles churned up, submerged, buried to the rhythm of each successive wave; a broken-up island

—with a saw-toothed shoreline; a swollen island—as if pregnant, the pyramidal shape of a dormant volcano; an island within an arc of fish and parrots; an island with austere points, sharp snail shells, mangrove thickets with a thousand hooks; an island surrounded by foam, like a little girl in a lace skirt; an island with the music of castanets and an island with roaring gorges; an island to run aground on, an island to be stranded on, an island with neither name nor history; an island where the wind sings through the cavities of enormous shells; an island with coral-like water flowers; an island with an inactive volcano; a moss-green island, a chalk-gray island, a salt-white island; islands in such a tight and sunny constellation—I have counted a hundred and four—that, thinking what to call them, I have named them *Gardens of the Queen* . . . Islands, islands, islands. More than five thousand islands, the Venetian chronicles tell us, surround the great kingdom of Cipango. So I must be approaching that great kingdom . . . And yet, as the days go by, I see the color of gold receding from me, because while the mineral keeps appearing, here, there, in the form of jewelry, figurines, beads, little bits—which are hardly ever even the size of a good Genoan hand—all of these are merely flecks, light traces, the barest hints of a great vein that has not yet appeared—and which was not found in Hispaniola, after all, as I had expected when I was under the illusion that it was an island of great riches. And now in my account of my second voyage, I begin to feel the need to make excuses. I sent word to Their Highnesses that I would have liked to have sent them a great quantity of gold, but I can't because my men have been stricken by so many diseases. I claim that what I have sent should be regarded only as *signs*. Because there is more: there is surely much more. And so I go on, searching, hoping, anxious, avid, and always more disillusioned, unable to find the source mine, the Mother Lode, the great bed, the supreme asset of these lands of spices without any spices . . . Now, in this house where it seems to be getting dark before it should, waiting for the confessor who should have been here by now, considering the closeness of the miserable little village where they've gone to look for him, I keep turning the pages of the drafts of my journals and letters. And viewing myself through words I wrote years ago, I observe, looking backward, that a diabolical change was taking place in my soul. Angered by those Indians who did not divulge their secret to me, who now hid their women when we arrived at their villages because there were among us some lewd and lascivious men; vexed by those mistrustful and insolent people who still, from time to time, shot arrows at us—although without doing us much harm to tell the truth—I stopped seeing them as kind, gentle, innocent beings, as incapable of malice as they were of seeing their nudity as shameful, which is the idyll I had painted for my sponsors when I returned from my first voyage. Now, more and more often, I call them *cannibals*—although I had never seen them eating human flesh. The India of spices has become for me the *India of Cannibals*. Not very dangerous cannibals—I insist—but cannibals who must not remain ignorant of our holy religion; cannibals whose souls must be saved (suddenly this becomes my obsession!), as millions of men and women in the pagan world were saved by the word of the Apostles of the Lord. But, since there is obviously no way of indoctrinating these cannibals, because we do not speak their languages, which I am discovering are many and distinct, the solution to this grave problem, which cannot be indifferent to the Church, is to take them to Spain as slaves. I have said: *as slaves*. Yes, now that I am at the gates of death the word appalls me, but in the account that I reread it is clearly written in my large, round hand. I requested a license for the *slave trade*. I maintained that the cannibals of these islands would be *better than any other slaves*, arguing, at the same time, that they can live on anything and that they eat much less than the blacks that are so numerous in Lisbon and Seville. (Since I cannot deliver gold, I think, I can substitute the irreplaceable energy of human flesh, a work force whose value lies in what it produces, which, in the final analysis, is of greater value than a mineral that comes in one hand and goes out the other...) Moreover, to prove my point, I sent several of those cannibals— whom I selected as the most able-bodied—along with *women, boys, and girls*, by ship to see how they would grow and reproduce in Spain, as had been done with the captives imported from Guinea. And I explained that with royal permission we could send caravels every year to obtain good shiploads of cannibals, whom we could deliver punctually in any quantity desired, hunting down the populations of the islands and keeping them in fenced camps until it was time to embark. And if it was objected that we lacked the manpower for such a task, I implored them to let me have some thousand men and a few hundred horses, so that I could begin tilling the earth and establishing wheat and grapes and grazing cattle. The people would have to be paid wages against the island's yields, but it was my thought— an ingenious plan of which I was disgracefully proud at the time —that they would not have to be paid in money: some stores would be set up in the royal hacienda to provide clothes, cheap shirts and jackets, handkerchiefs, coats, trousers, and shoes, as well as medicines, cures and miscellaneous pharmaceuticals, *surplus* goods and Spanish products that *the people here would accept gratefully to alleviate their misery.* (In short, they would be paid in our goods, which would be a profitable arrangement, since they would never see a penny, and, anyway, money would do them little good, they would quickly incur lifelong debts, signing for their purchases . . .) Considering, however, that the roundup of slaves that I proposed would be sure to meet with some resistance on the part of the cannibals, I requested—a prepared man is as good as two—the shipment of *two hundred cuirasses, one hundred muskets, and a hundred crossbows*, along with the materials necessary to maintain and repair them . . . And I concluded my catalog of shameful proposals, written in Isabella City on the thirtieth of January, 1496, by begging God to give me *one good deposit of gold*—as if I had not fallen, on that day, into His disfavor, by initiating the slave trade. (Instead of begging His pardon and doing penance, miserable one, I asked him for *one good deposit of gold*, the way a whore asks each day, facing the uncertain and long night ahead of her, to be favored by the providential apparition of a splendid and careless person with a free hand and a heavy purse! . . .)

Michele de Cuneo

Slave Trading with Columbus

In this passage Columbus's compatriate Michele de Cuneo presents a cold-blooded account of the ruthlessness of the slave trade conducted by the discoverer.

When our caravels were to leave for Spain, we gathered in our settlement one thousand six hundred male and female persons of these Indians, and of these we embarked in our caravels on February 17, 1495, five hundred fifty souls among the healthiest males and females. For those who remained, we let it be known in the vicinity that anyone who wanted to take some of them could do so, to the amount desired; which was done. And when each man was thus provided with slaves, there still remained about four hundred, to whom permission was granted to go where they wished. Among them were many women with children still at suck. Since they were afraid that we might return to capture them once again, and in order to escape us the better, they left their children anywhere on the ground and began to flee like desperate creatures; and some fled so far that they found themselves at seven or eight days' distance from our community at Isabela, beyond the mountains and across enormous rivers; consequently, they will henceforth be captured only with great difficulty.

Bartolomé de Las Casas

Raiding the Bahamas

Bartolomé de Las Casas's major works are the most important source of our knowledge about the early colonial period in the Indies. He initially came to America as an adventurer in 1502; later he became a Dominican priest and composed the fullest history of the Indies. Our debt to Las Casas is enormous. He preserved the journal of Columbus's first voyage and other documents, to which he added his own detailed observations and memories. Carl Sauer considers Las Casas one of America's greatest historians and geographers, declaring that "no one knew the country [Hispaniola] and its natives so well and so long." Alastair Reid calls him "an extraordinarily observant and intelligent presence."

Here Las Casas provides an eyewitness account of the rapacity that led to the depopulation of the Bahamas. Within a few years of their discovery, the main islands of Cuba and Hispaniola had suffered a drastic decline in population. The Spanish had to obtain slaves elsewhere. They would be brought from Africa.

The first Spaniards who engaged in the slave trade—so the story goes—knew of the simple and trusting nature of the islanders, which had so impressed the Admiral on his first encounters with them, when they had shown him their generosity. When the first two ships landed there, the islanders thought (before experience taught them better) that the people aboard had come from Heaven and so gave them a fitting welcome. Our people told the islanders that they had come from Hispaniola where the souls of the Indians' dead ancestors and loved ones were living in peace; and that if the Indians wished to visit them the Spaniards would take them there on their ships. (All these Indian peoples believe that souls are immortal, that after people die their souls live on in wonderful places where all their wants are satisfied; although some believe that the souls must suffer first to pay for the sins they committed in this life.)

The first Spaniards who arrived there—so the story goes—used this vile deception to entice the unsuspecting islanders. Men and women flocked on board the ships, bringing their clothes and household goods and stores of food from their gardens. On Hispaniola, it was not the souls of their ancestors and the people they loved that met them, but iron picks and shovels, iron levers and crowbars, and other similar tools—and in the mines they were forced to work with these tools, mines where life was short for them. Full of despair at finding themselves duped, they poisoned themselves with yucca juice; or died of hunger and overwork, delicate as they were, peoples that had never imagined having to undergo such hardships.

Later the raiders used other tricks and stratagems to entrap the Indians. None escaped. When the ships full of Indians landed, usually at Puerto de Plata and Puerto Real on the north coast opposite the Lucayas, the Indians were unloaded and divided into lots, according to the amount of money that had been put up by the traders: the old with the young, the sick with the healthy (for many fell ill at sea and even died of hunger, thirst, and the crowded and overheated conditions below decks). In dividing the lots, no attempt was made to allow wives and husbands to stay together, nor parents and children, for the Indians were treated as if they were the lowest of animals. . . .

On one occasion about seven thousand Indians had been collected on a small island, with seven Spaniards guarding them, as if they were so many ewes and lambs. They were there for quite some time waiting for the ships that would carry them off, and their food ran out. Eventually two ships arrived, carrying cassava (that was all the Indians were ever given to eat; if other food was available it was reserved for the Spaniards). As the ships were nearing the island, a terrible storm arose, and the ships were broken up and foundered. The seven thousand Indians and the seven Spaniards all died of hunger. I do not remember what happened to the people on the ships. None of the Spanish adventurers thought of the daily judgements of God, nor saw such disasters as a punishment for their sins; instead they considered them as no more than bad luck, as if there were no Lord in Heaven watching their acts and bringing them to account for the harsh injustices they committed. I could tell innumerable stories of the crimes and atrocities committed against these poor sheep while I was on the island, stories I heard from the very men who committed them.

Bartolomé de Las Casas

God's Word Uproots Idolatry

In addition to his historical observations, Bartolomé de Las Casas also interprets the conquest and casts judgement upon it. His will predicts that "because of these impious, criminal and ignominious deeds perpetrated so unjustly, tyrannically and barbarously, God will vent on Spain His wrath and His fury, for nearly all of Spain has shared in the bloody wealth usurped at the cost of so much ruin and slaughter."

Las Casas was an activist; his was the first voice raised to demand the humane treatment of the Indians.

And yet Las Casas approved the importation of slaves from Africa.

God's word, by its admirable power, touches the hearts of any people, no matter how wild they may be, rooting out idolatry and every other vice. And His word has a much greater effect on the Indians then upon any other people, since the Indians are much gentler and meeker than most of the world's peoples and are well known for their docility and their great receptivity and readiness to receive the faith. I know this from my own experience, and for the greater glory of Christ I am recording what I have seen with my own eyes over a period of fifty years, a candid account intended for posterity.

The Spaniards boldly entered this New World, a land that was unknown in past centuries. Once here, they disobeyed their Lord and committed enormous and extraordinary crimes: they massacred uncounted thousands of Indians, scattered their flocks, burned their villages, razed their cities: without any justification, or even any pretext of justification, the Spaniards did horrible and shameful things to a suffering people. Fierce, rapacious, and cruel, could the Spaniards have had any knowledge of the one true God being revealed to the Indians by our priests?

Fray Antonio de Montesinos

The First American
Sermon Against Exploitation

This impassioned plea by a Dominican friar was delivered in 1511 to a congregation of Spaniards at Santo Domingo, in the thatch-roofed log building that served as their church. Transcribed by Bartolomé de Las Casas, it is the first recorded protest by a European in America. Eduardo Galeano (himself a voice of protest and courage) imagines the response: "We'll denounce you to King Ferdinand! You'll be deported!" But Galeano also pictures a lone dissident spirit among the congregation: "One bewildered man remains silent," he writes in MEMORY OF FIRE: GENESIS. *"He came to these lands nine years ago. Owner of Indians, gold mines, and plantations, he has made a small fortune. His name is Bartolomé de Las Casas, and he will soon be the first priest ordained in the New World."*

This little sermon by a humble friar may have inspired the great work of Las Casas. A small voice raised in the service of truth and justice may be a force beyond anyone's awareness or understanding.

Tell me by what right, by what law do you keep these Indians in such cruel, such horrible bondage? By what authority have you waged such detestable wars against these peoples, who lived quietly and peacefully on land that was their own? Wars in which you have destroyed incalculable numbers of them by homicide and slaughters surpassing anything in history? Why do you keep them so oppressed and exhausted, not giving them enough to eat, not curing the illness they develop from the excessive labor you force upon them, so that they pass away—no you murder them!—in order to extract and obtain gold every single day?

What effort do you make to instruct them in religion, so that they may know their God and creator, be baptized, hear mass, and observe Sundays and holy days? Are they not men? Do they not have souls capable of reason? Are you not bound to love them as you love yourselves? Why can't you comprehend this? Why can't you feel this? Why are you lost in this deep, lethargic sleep? Rest assured, in this state you can no more be saved than the Moors or the Turks, who do not have faith in Jesus Christ and do not desire it.

Pope Paul III

They Are People

The Spanish debate about the Indians' humanity was officially ended by Pope Paul III's decisive proclamation of 1537, in which he declared them to be human beings, with the liberties and responsibilities of all people (including the responsibility to embrace the Christian faith).

Unfortunately, the pope's ruling did not put an end to the slave economy in America.

Truth itself, which can neither deceive nor be deceived, when it appointed the preachers of faith to the office of preaching, is well known to have said: "Go, teach all nations." He said *all* without any distinction, for all are capable of receiving the instruction of the faith. The enemy of mankind who always opposes good undertakings in order to bring them to nought, aware of this commission, and instigated by envy, invented a method hitherto unknown of preventing the Word of God from being preached to the nations that they might be saved. . . . He has excited some of his satellites who, eagerly desiring to satisfy their avarice, habitually presume to assert that the western and southern Indians and the other nations which in these times have come to our knowledge . . . should, like brutes, be brought under our servitude.

And indeed, they are made slaves and treated with an inhumanity that their masters would scarcely exercise over the very brutes that serve them.

We, therefore, who, though unworthy, are the viceregent of our Lord upon earth, and who seek with our whole endeavor the sheep of his flock entrusted to us and who are outside the fold, in order to bring them into the fold itself, reflecting that these Indians as true men are not only capable of the Christian faith, but also—as has been made known to us—that they embrace the faith with the utmost promptitude, and wishing to provide them with suitable remedies, decree and declare by apostolical authority:

That the above-mentioned Indians and all other nations who may in future come to the knowledge of Christians, though they be out of the faith of Christ, can freely and lawfully use, possess and enjoy their liberty in that regard. And that they ought not to be reduced to slavery. And that whatever may otherwise have been done is null and void.

Moreover, that those Indians and other nations are to be invited to the aforesaid faith of Christ by the Preaching of the Word of God and by the example of a good life.

This decree is to hold good, notwithstanding any previous acts and whatsoever else to the contrary.

Malcolm Margolin

In a California Mission

Clerics like Bartolomé de Las Casas, despite opposing the violence and brutality of the conquistadores, have not themselves escaped criticism from Native Americans. In California, where many Spanish missions are preserved as historic monuments, schoolchildren each year make elaborate models of these lovely communities. The realities of hardship, oppression, and resistance are not emphasized.

One of the first and best outside reports of mission life was that of Jean François de La Pérouse, who visited the Monterey mission in 1786. Malcolm Margolin, in his introduction to a portion of La Pérouse's JOURNALS published under the title MONTEREY IN 1786, describes Indian life in the missions based on contemporaneous reports.

A passage from "Mission Studies and the Columbian Quincentennial," an article by Native American Studies professor Edward D. Castillo that originally appeared in NEWS FROM NATIVE AMERICA, provides a fitting introduction to this selection.

> *For years, California schoolchildren have been presented with a nostalgic, rose-tinted picture of gentle, brown-robed Franciscans bringing deprived and primitive Indians to the missions to learn an orderly, wholesome, agricultural way of life. This picture fades fast in the light of examination, but some scholars have zealously attempted to preserve it with selective readings of history, completely*

overlooking the suffering of Indian people, and oblivious to the sound-
ness and validity of Indian ways of life.

Adding insult to injury is the recent campaign to make the founder
of the California missions, Junipero Serra, a saint. What makes that
effort so offensive are allegations by supporters that degrade and
ridicule native California cultures, characterizing them as brutish
and savage.

Fortunately, other scholars are now being listened to; the voices
of criticism and reflection are heard even within the Church. Also
fortunately, a significant number of responsible public agencies and
scholars are attempting to use the forthcoming five-hundredth anni-
versary of the Columbian voyages to the Americas as a forum for
thoughtful reflection upon the meaning of that event to the people
living today, including California Indians. . . .

The unrelenting efforts of the missionaries produced virtually
unrelenting misery for the Indians. Unable to rebel, their old
way of life destroyed, they sank into the deepest gloom. The
heavy depression that hung over Mission Carmel hung over other
California missions as well, and La Pérouse was not alone in
describing it. "I have never seen one laugh," wrote Louis Choris
about the Indians of Mission Dolores in San Francisco. "They
look as though they were interested in nothing."

"A deep melancholy always clouds their faces, and their eyes
are constantly fixed upon the ground," wrote Otto von Kotzebue,
also of Mission Dolores. Captain Vancouver likewise noted that
"all operations and functions both of body and mind appeared to
be carried out with a mechanical, lifeless, careless indifference."

The missions of California were places of defeat and death—
not only physical death, but cultural and spiritual death as well.
This conclusion is unavoidable from reading what La Pérouse
and others have said, and it is supported by what we can further
deduce by reading carefully between the lines. La Pérouse mentions, for example, that the hair of the Indians was singed short.
The cropping and singeing of hair was not a customary fashion
among the Indians, but used only as a sign of mourning. The
fact that La Pérouse presents it as a general style suggests the
prevalence of death, the fact that he was seeing an entire culture
in mourning.

La Pérouse also mentions that many children had hernias and were dying because of them. He points to this as an example of the low level of medical skill among the Spaniards who were unable to treat simple hernias successfully. But for us there is the larger question of what kind of overwork or mistreatment of children there must have been at the missions to have produced so many hernias, an ailment which seems to have been relatively uncommon before the coming of the Spaniards.

Then, too, La Pérouse provides us with a shocking description of how the Indians were butchering a cow, eating the meat raw, and croaking like ravens with pleasure when they found fat. La Pérouse assumes that this was a typical example of the Indians' uncivilized manners, but that was hardly the case. In fact, traditionally people were expected to show restraint in all things, especially eating, and good manners demanded that one express little interest in the food that was offered. The scene of people falling upon a butchered cow and eating it raw suggests something akin to—if not starvation—at least severe malnourishment. Indeed, from La Pérouse's description of their general diet we might assume that the Indians at Mission Carmel were desperate for protein and fat.

The overwork, the hours of forced prayer (in Latin), the deadening of sensibilities and intelligence, the whippings, the remorseless tedium of daily routine, the utter hopelessness—all these things led La Pérouse, however reluctantly, to conclude that the mission resembled nothing so much as a slave plantation of Santo Domingo.

Eduardo Galeano

Feet

This excerpt from Eduardo Galeano's MEMORY OF FIRE: GENESIS *is based on an incident described in Oviedo's* GENERAL AND NATURAL HISTORY OF THE INDIES. *Everything about it is shocking, but what may be most shocking is the date that it occurred:* 1522. *Only thirty years after Columbus discovered paradise, black slaves are working the mills of Hispaniola. Here the first of many black revolts is brutally suppressed.*

The rebellion, the first by black slaves in America, has been smashed. It had broken out in the sugar mills of Diego Columbus, the son of the discoverer. Fire had spread through the mills and plantations of the whole island. The blacks had risen up with the few surviving Indians, armed with sticks and stones and sugar-cane lances that broke against armor in futile fury.

Now from the gallows scattered along the highways hang women and men, the young and old. At the traveler's eye level dangle feet by which he can guess what the victims were before death came. Among these leathery limbs, gashed by toil and tread, are frisky feet and formal feet; prisoner feet and feet that still dance, loving the earth and calling for war.

Eduardo Galeano

The Eighth Wonder of the World

The "silver mountain" of Potosí in Bolivia was considered the richest source of silver in the world at the dawn of the seventeenth century. Eduardo Galeano paints a vivid picture of the contrast between the opulence its silver purchased and the hellish lives of the Indians who mined it.

Caravans of llamas and mules carry to the port of Arica the silver that the Potosí mountain bleeds from each of its mouths. At the end of a long voyage the ingots arrive in Europe to finance war, peace and progress there.

In exchange, from Seville or by contraband, Potosí receives the wines of Spain, the hats and silks of France, the lace, mirrors, and tapestry of Flanders, German swords, Genoese paper, Neapolitan stockings, Venetian glass, Cypriot wax, Ceylonese diamonds, East Indian marbles, the perfumes of Arabia, Malacca, and Goa, Persian carpets and Chinese porcelain, black slaves from Cape Verde and Angola, and dashing steeds from Chile.

Everything is very dear in this city, the dearest in the world. Only *chicha* corn liquor and coca leaves are cheap. The Indians, forcibly seized from the communities of all Peru, spend Sundays in the corrals dancing to their drums and drinking *chicha* till they roll on the ground. On Monday mornings they are herded into the mountain and, chewing coca and beaten with iron bars, they pursue the veins of silver, greenish-white serpents that appear and take flight through the entrails of this immense paunch, no light, no air. There the Indians toil all week, prisoners, breathing dust that kills the lungs, and chewing coca that deceives hunger and masks exhaustion, never knowing when night falls or day breaks, until Saturday ends and the bell rings for prayer and release. Then they move forward, holding lighted candles, to emerge on Sunday at dawn, so deep are the diggings and the infinite tunnels and galleries.

A priest newly come to Potosí sees them arriving in the city's suburbs, a long procession of squalid ghosts, their backs scarred by the lash, and remarks: "I don't want to see this portrait of hell."

"So shut your eyes," someone suggests.

"I can't," he says. "With my eyes shut I see more."

Alice Walker

The Form of My Brokenness

In THE TEMPLE OF MY FAMILIAR *the opposition between self and other described by Todorov as providing the motive force in the conquest of the New World takes the form of a mythic history of the earth, centering around a shifting balance of power between men and women. For this reason Alice Walker describes her novel as "a romance of the last 500,000 years." In the novel the ancestor stories of Indian and black women, stories from the "old, old days . . . when only women had been priests . . . and the earth was a large woman, a goddess," are opposed to individual stories of the suffering of the oppressed during the days of the slave trade, when "the white man, in his dual role of spiritual guide and religious prostitute . . . by making the Bible say whatever was necessary to keep his plantation going, and using it as a tool to degrade women and enslave blacks . . . made himself the sole conduit to God, if not at times the actual God* himself." *The slave trade as depicted here expands the pattern of individual rape to become a symbol of the rape of Mother Africa and Mother Earth.*

While the novel as a whole provides a vision of this male / female opposition overcome in a sexual healing, in the passage quoted here both masters and slaves are "shamed and degraded" by the slave society. Here a pair of Indian lovers in Latin America are annihilated and the physical

and emotional torment of the slave is revealed. "I was broken," the nar-
rator says, "utterly: in that I could trust no one, that I could never
again reach out to love. . . ."

"They called him Jesús," whispered Zedé, clutching Arveyda's
hand, though her back remained turned to him, "because they
would not have been able to pronounce his real name even if he
had told them what it was, which he did not, and he was a slave
like the rest of us. Only, it was his own village in which we were
kept. They also called him 'indio loco' because everyone else from
his tribe had run away but he could not run away. He would run
a little away and hide out in the jungle, which he knew intimately,
just as the animals knew it. He had always been there, you
know. There was no time in his life when he had not been there
on that piece of earth. So he would hide, and then he would sneak
back and walk about the village in the dead of night. Nothing
would be stolen, not even food, and this was very puzzling to
everyone, our enslavers and ourselves alike.

"The reason he came back, a reason our enslavers never knew
and would not have understood anyhow, was that he was the
protector of the sacred stones of the village. These stones were
three simple, ordinary-looking rocks that must always be in a
certain area of the village's center. If no one ever told you they
were special, believe me you'd never know it. They blended into
the earth perfectly. And yet, once Jesús had pointed them out
to me, and showed me the sacred configuration, which was the
same as the nuclear-bomb-shelter symbol, the stones leaped out
at me, and I was hard-pressed to be silent when they were kicked
about or simply trod upon. When they were kicked, as by the
soldiers in their sullen idleness, or when some poor soul was
beaten and blood was spilled upon them, or when a morsel of
food that someone dropped touched them—well! This meant
another definite visit from Jesús, who would have to risk life and
limb to restore the stones' position, wash off the blood, brush off
the food, and so on. When I knew him better, I knew it would
never have occurred to him to save himself if it meant abandoning

his duty to the three small stones—about the size and color of brown pigeon eggs. As a dog is inevitably drawn back to where a bone is buried, Jesús returned to the stones. The keeping of them was his whole life, and it had been for thousands of years! He fully believed that if the stones were not kept, his people, the Krapokechuan, or 'human beings,' would remain dispersed forever and never again find a home. Because where the stones were was their home, you understand. Nowhere else. It is something not understood by norteamericanos; this I know.

"At last they captured him. How sorry we were! For though most of us were ashamed of the Indian part of ourselves, his presence was like that of a guardian spirit, an angel, and the times we managed to glimpse him, as he stole through the village at odd hours of the night, convinced us he was indeed wholly benign. He was so young! With a bush of hair to his waist. He wore only a cloth around his loins and beautiful red parrot feathers in his ears.

"Our captors did not understand his language, and when they beat him he was silent. They made him work with the rest of us, clearing the forest with a machete. The men used machetes and pickaxes and saws to fell and uproot the trees and vines, and the women used hoes and rakes to complete the slaughter of the earth. This was our work, day in, day out, from the crow of a rooster at dawn until dark. The guards forced the women to mate with them, and before long each guard had chosen his favorite slave 'wife.' The one who chose me did not force me, but bided his time. He was someone who beat and burned and killed without emotion or remorse, yet still managed to cling to the belief that someone would want to sleep with him without the use of force. It was a matter of pride to him. I only knew I was chosen because of how he looked at me and because the other men left me alone, and I would often hear their slave women screaming or sobbing prayers into the night.

"I did not plan to love Jesús. But how unlike them he was! There is in me, deep, always somewhere, the love of the priest, but the *true* priest, the one who watches over, the one who protects. Above all, the one who is more than his fancy dress. If there is any spirit that I find wholly erotic it is that one. *Aiiee!* Jesús was such a priest I used to feel as if the trees fell before him to be blessed, because, clearly, cutting them down was for him a torture comparable to being cut down himself. They were sobbing all the while, Jesús and his trees. He had known them his whole life. And for all his lifetimes before.

"Like it was with us, querido, I did not know what was happening or what to do about it. His eyes spoke. My womb leaped. Don't laugh! Though expressed in the language of imbeciles, this is the way it was! We discovered I knew a few words of his strange language. The word for water, 'ataras,' the word for wood, 'xotmea,' the word for love, 'oooo.' The word for love, truly, *four* o's! They could not watch us every minute. During an hour they could not witness and will never own, I made love to him. He made love to me. We made love together. They had bound him by the feet so that he could not move his legs apart. I crept into his hut and without speaking caressed and kissed him for a long time before taking him into my mouth. When I placed myself on top of him he was crying, and I was crying, and he held one of my breasts in my mouth, and his damp hair was like a warm fog on my face. *Ai,* they will never own passion!

"The second, and last, time was like the first, only even more intense. I knew the instant Carlotta was conceived. The seed flew into me where I was so open, and I fell off Jesús already asleep. It was asleep together that they found us. The first thing he did, the guard that had chosen me to want to sleep with him, was to cut off Jesús' hair. He did it slowly, coldly, methodically, as if he had been thinking of doing it for a long time. He did it with a very sharp machete, and when the long, thick, rough black hair covered his dusty boots, he stamped his feet free of it as if stamping out desire.

"He never touched me himself, not even to beat me. That night the other men, the guards, one after another came to the little hut in the forest in which they placed me. While this was happening to me, they killed Jesús. At dawn, as I lay bleeding, they brought his body and threw it in with me. Then they nailed shut the door, which was the only opening. Jesús' throat had been cut. They had also removed his genitals. He had been violated in every conceivable way. There was not even a scrap of cloth to cover him. I was naked.

"Days and nights went by. The flies came by the hundreds. The rats. The smell. I beat on the door until my hands, covered with flies also, were dripping blood. I screamed. There were only the jungle sounds outside. I had nightmares, when I could sleep, about the body of the man I had loved. He was so silent. I cursed him now for being the death of me.

"And then one night I heard a noise outside the door—soft, almost not a noise. And then the door slowly opened, and the mournful and barbaric-looking tribesmen of Jesús filled the little hut. They wrapped his body in a large blanket before they turned to me, naked, shivering, dying on the dirt floor. Then I saw there was also a blanket for me.

"I would have stayed with them if I could. They understood, as no one else ever would, the form of my brokenness. I was broken, utterly: in that I could trust no one, that I could never again reach out to love, that it must be brought to me. But they were always on the run, and the soldiers always after them. When Carlotta was born, they made me understand I must go away in order to save her, in order to save Jesús. They took me to a house where there were Indians living the way the gringo lets Indians live; they were all busy making trinkets for the tourist dollar, of which the white man who controlled and 'protected' them from the soldiers got the largest share. They hid me and my baby. I learned to make their vivid green pottery. Since I knew Spanish, I helped the women hawk their wares on the streets of a not-too-distant town, full of the well-to-do descendants of the Spanish conquistadors and the blank-eyed americanos. I did not earn anything beyond enough for food. My friends told me of a school run by gringos where I might be able to get a job as a maidslave. That was the beginning of my flight to Norte America.

"My parting from Jesús' people was one the rest of the world will never see, nor will they understand its meaning. I am not sure I understand its meaning myself. I only know that they gave me the last remaining symbols of who they were in the world— feathers from the red African parrot for my ears, this parrot that had been brought to their village so many hundreds of years ago by the men with rough hair, from a continent they called Zuma, or Sun, and they gave me, for Carlotta, the three pigeon-egg-size stones."

Eduardo Galeano

Freedom

In this excerpt from MEMORY OF FIRE: GENESIS, *a slave escapes to join others in the free communities at Palmares in Brazil. Palmares had been the home of the Caeté Indians, who, like the Tainos encountered by Columbus, had been exterminated by the Europeans. But the fugitives survived and thrived. Escaped slaves from many African cultures, communicating through the Portuguese of their former masters, created a new community, growing corn, beans, and other crops and raising pigs and chickens.*

Palmares is a symbol of hope. The conquest of America helped to create the multicultural society that exists in this hemisphere today. We agree with Tzvetan Todorov that our best hope lies in learning to recognize equality in difference.

The hounds' braying and the slave-hunters' trumpeting have long since faded away. The fugitive crosses a field of stubble, fierce stubble higher then himself, and runs toward the river.

He throws himself on the grass, face down, arms open, legs wide apart. He hears the accomplice voices of the grasshoppers and cicadas and little frogs. "I am not a thing. My history is not the history of things." He kisses the earth, bites it. "I got my foot out of the trap. I'm not a thing." He presses his naked body to the dew-soaked ground and hears the sound of small plants coming through the earth, eager to be born. He is mad with hunger, and for the first time hunger gives him happiness. His body is covered with cuts, and he does not feel it. He turns toward the sky as if embracing it. The moon rises and strikes him, violent blows of light from the full moon and juicy stars, and he gets up and looks for his direction.

Now for the jungle. Now for the green screen of greenness.

"You heading for Palmares, too?" the fugitive asks an ant crawling up his hand. "Guide me."

Kirkpatrick Sale

The Conquest of Paradise

Kirkpatrick Sale, from whom we have already quoted often, is a founder of the New York Green Party. In this passage from THE CONQUEST OF PARADISE: CHRISTOPHER COLUMBUS AND THE COLUMBIAN LEGACY, *he discusses the European attitude toward the land—the destruction caused not only by greed but also by heedlessness.*

As heedless as they were of the people of the islands, the Spanish invaders were even more careless, and nearly as destructive, of the islands themselves.

It was the Admiral's design all along, and it seemed only natural to the Sovereigns, to export Castilian life to the Indies and to turn Española, as its name suggested, into a Spanish island, with Spanish livestock, Spanish crops, Spanish food and drink. We can tell, by the extent of provisioning records and the commentaries of the early travelers, that no thought was given to whether the foreign life-forms belonged in the islands, whether they would prosper, whether they would damage the native species: it simply was assumed that anything the Europeans wanted to grow would and should grow. An appreciation of the differences of natural environments and the fragility of established ecosystems was not, apparently, for all their classical learning and Renaissance scientism, something the minds of Europe took with them abroad; as long as there was land there, neither native populations nor native species were regarded as any barrier to implantation. "The European," in [biologist Alfred W.] Crosby's words, "immediately set out to transform as much of the New World as possible into the Old World."

The first species that Colón chose to import were those that made up the staples of the Mediterranean diet (psychologically, anyway)—chickpeas, wheat, wine, and olive oil. The wheat and chickpeas withered in the heat—"at the most [they] grow nine inches," Cuneo noted in his letter, "then all at once they wilt and dry": the vines produced sparse and stunted grape clusters out of which no liquid could be pressed; the olive trees wouldn't take at all. (The general response to that was well expressed by the Spanish cleric who argued some years later that since these forsaken lands couldn't produce the wine necessary for the celebration of the Lord's sacrament, He obviously hadn't meant their inhabitants to become Christians in the first place.) Other European plants did rather better—cauliflowers and cabbages, melons, cucumbers, and radishes—but the attempt to change the environment to suit the European diet was never successful, and instead the colonists decided to rely on imports from the homeland; hardly any thought was given—I know of none on record—to trying to change the diet to suit the environment. This was in large part responsible for the recurrent famines that affected Europeans on Española from the start: not that there was not enough food—that couldn't be, with the productivity of the *conuco* system—but that it wasn't *Castilian* food and Ysla Española wasn't Spain. Even during those periods of famine when they came perforce to depend on Taino food grown and supplied by Tainos amid all the hardships, the Spanish absorbed only the smallest elements of it into their regular diets, regarding it as somehow, well, *foreign*.

Despite the spotty beginning, the Spanish, under Colón and well into the sixteenth century, introduced a whole range of European animal and plant species, intentionally and inadvertently, with severe and ultimately near-ruinous effect. It hardly mattered whether the new species were benign or malignant:

the more they adapted themselves to their new environment the more they displaced the native species, the more they altered and eventually transformed the long-stable ecosystem of the islands.

Take, for instance, the large European mammals that were brought over on the Second Voyage. Nothing of the kind (nothing larger than a small dog) lived in the Caribbean, no competing species of any sort, so there were no established diseases to threaten them and, with the exception of sheep and goats, they bloomed spectacularly. Cattle reproduced so successfully on Española that, it was said, thirty or forty stray animals would multiply to three or four hundred in a couple of years; horses did so well—a lucky thing for the Castilian *caballeros* there—that the original twenty had multiplied to at least sixty or seventy within a decade and by 1507 imports of horses were forbidden; pigs were so numerous by 1500, just seven years after the first four pairs were introduced, that according to Las Casas they were called *infinitos.*

All these voracious animals naturally dominated and then destroyed native habitats, rapidly and thoroughly, with human help and without. The record is inadequate, since none of the colonists, even those who would take on the job of describing native species for audiences at home, ever noted the extensive alteration of the environment that was taking place literally beneath their feet. Las Casas, however, does mention that a certain grass common in Española at the turn of the century had vanished just forty years later, a victim of the hungry herds, and we may presume there were many similar floral die-outs. Crosby, without specifics, considers that the spread of these large species "doubtlessly had much to do with the extinction of certain plants, animals . . . and even the Indians themselves" who lost out "in the biological competition with the newly imported livestock."

Typical of this process was the *ranchero* system that Colón imported wholesale from Castile—complete with roundups, lassos, open ranges, branding, and cowboys on horseback—and installed with herds of 500 head or more (and by the 1520s, according to Oviedo, some of 8,000 or more). These stocks were let loose everywhere, in fields abandoned because of depopulation, in valleys cleared of forest cover, in native *conuco* farms, even on steep hillside slopes; everywhere they depleted the native grass species, compacted the tropical soils, and stripped the ground cover that had resisted soil erosion. Thus here, in its very first New World outpost, Europe implanted a system, and endowed a legacy, that would go on to mark indelibly both of the continents it was to conquer—and would produce a red-meat-dependent society that almost automatically ensured environmental destruction.

In addition to the invasive animals, the plants introduced by the Spanish had a deleterious effect. These included the ones established accidentally—such aggressive pioneer species as daisies and dandelions and nettles that moved into any open space and crowded out the weaker native species—as well as those that were deliberately introduced and fostered, such as sugar, brought in from the Canaries, which took immediately to the Caribbean climate and was rapidly installed in all lands not given over to food and livestock. Again, though we know with precision what invader species established themselves in the islands, we have a very imperfect record of the species that were lost: none of the contemporary chroniclers noted them, and despite the "obviously . . . spectacular biogeographical phenomenon going on right under their noses," they "did not understand it," Crosby says, and certainly did not take the trouble to write about it.

Not just the *kinds* of plants but the *system* of planting: the European style of intensive agriculture, particularly row-style plantation agriculture that the Spanish established everywhere, was the worst sort to introduce to a tropical ecosystem. It was done by plowing, which laid soil to waste far more severely than the Indians' planting stick and hoe; it used monocultural open-field planting, which exposed the surface soils to wind and water erosion far more drastically than the Tainos' careful *conuco* planting; and it required (along with fuel and shelter needs) the cutting and almost complete clearing of the heavy evergreen forests that were the stable, old-growth vegetation throughout the Caribbean.

The inevitable results of this were noticeable within a few

decades. Soils were quickly eroded by the torrential rains and fierce winds of what the Tainos called *hurricana*, with attendant loss of nutrients and organisms; rivers began to silt up and in some cases went completely dry; estuarine habitats were destroyed by siltation and estuarine animals disappeared; and with the loss of the dense tree cover the whole hydrology, and thus the whole climate, of the area was slowly altered, at considerable cost to both land and water species. Interestingly, Colón himself was astutely aware of this last point, realizing the importance of the forests for local climate: he had noted on his trip to Cuba in 1494 that "in the Canary, Madeira, and Azore Islands . . . since the removal of forests that once covered those islands, they do not have so much mist and rain as before," and again in 1498 wrote of the Cape Verde Islands that they "have a very misleading name, for Colón [Columbus] himself never saw a single green thing; everything was dry and sterile." This wisdom, however, had no influence on the agricultural policies he permitted in Española, in which deforestation played a major part.

Just two decades after the tenure of Governor Colón, in 1518, Alonso de Zuaso wrote to a friend at the Spanish court, "If I were to tell you all the damage that has been done, I should never make an end. . . . Although these islands had been, since God made the earth, prosperous and full of people lacking nothing they needed; yet . . . they were laid waste, inhabited only by wild animals and birds, and useless indeed for the service of either God or of Their Highnesses." Las Casas would add, some years later, of Española: "It was the first to be destroyed and made into a desert." But not the last.

Michael Dorris & Louise Erdrich

The Crown of Columbus

Michael Dorris and Louise Erdrich's THE CROWN OF COLUMBUS *tells the tale of a hunt for "the greatest treasure in Christendom," a crown awarded Columbus for his discovery. Among those searching for the crown (which may be read as representing the legacy of Columbus) are Vivian Twostar, an anthropologist of Native American descent; her lover Roger Williams, a poet "who had built a career on poeticizing history"; and Henry Cobb, an avaricious and ruthless businessman, "the closest living representation of Columbus himself." In this passage, narrated by Vivian's teenage son, the crown is discovered at last—but it is not what was expected (also present are Hilda and Racine, scholar friends of Vivian, and her infant daughter, Violet). "I thought it was my salvation," Cobb comments. Instead "it was a gift of poison, a treasure fit to be dug only so that it could be put away. Like so much Columbus had carried, it was a curse."*

`e ne ya . . . a beautiful one came into my hands, a beautiful one came into my hands, `a `a `a.

Now I am long life, now happiness as a beautiful one came into my hands.
Before me it is blessed as a beautiful one came into my hands.
Behind me it is blessed as a beautiful one came into my hands.
Below me it is blessed as a beautiful one came into my hands.
Above me it is blessed as a beautiful one came into my hands.

Around me it is blessed as a beautiful one came into my hands.
My speech is blessed as a beautiful one came into my hands.
My surroundings are blessed when a beautiful one came into my hands.
A beautiful one came into my hands.

Things come together sometimes, they connect, and when that happens it feels right. No Navajo had been anywhere near Eleuthera long ago, but somehow these were the words that should be said. They came back when they needed to. Roger hadn't understood a bit of what Mom spoke, but he stood with his head bowed, the way you do in a strange church when you want to show respect. Hilda looked fascinated, as though she couldn't wait to know more, and Racine . . . it's funny but he looked like he was praying himself. His lips were silently moving, forming words I couldn't read. Violet, for her part, had the decency to stay asleep.

Before Mom was done she had made a strategy, and took charge.

"Feed it to me," she instructed Roger and Racine, then reeled in the net as their grips retreated across it. The heaviness of the box made a depression in the web, but as long as we kept the tension even, there was no way it could fall through. And we were careful. In the process each of us retreated a few steps onto firmer ground. The circumference got wider, and we didn't let go until what had been the center was moved to the edge. Watching all those circles in the circles of circles was like looking down the mouth of a telescope while the focus got more and more precise and every sight but one was funnelled out. By the time it was safe, the box was all we saw. Before it touched the ground I said the two lines of the "Way" I like the best because sometimes they seemed to describe better than anything else how I felt.

Now I am the boy-reared-at-the-interior-of-mirage, I found mirage, *ni yo o*.
At the center of the mirage I found mirage.

It was glass carpeted with dung and there was something inside its walls. We knelt and squinted our eyes to see within, but the angles of vision were tight and narrow. From one vantage I made out part of something straight and from another, the curve of something round. Roger picked it up, held it like a prism to the disappearing sun. It turned his face red, but still he couldn't decipher the contents.

"Murano crystal, I would guess," Racine observed when Roger set the box down. "Very old and made by a master. It's a treasure."

"It's just a *container*," Mom corrected. "Inside is what we came here for, what Peter Paul, that long-ago Mohawk at Dartmouth, hid for me to find."

"There are no seams." Roger examined the box slowly, looking for some point of entry. "It's as if it were blown whole around . . . whatever."

"A ship in a bottle," I said. "But no cork."

"So the question is, what do we do?" Hilda was practical. For her, there were always choices. Either we took the thing unopened, or we found a way to penetrate it here.

"It should be studied under optimal conditions," Racine argued. "Each step should be documented, photographed. It should go to the Smithsonian or to the British Museum."

"One could make the case," Hilda went on, "that it belongs to Cobb. I've read about these suits of ownership. Persistence counts in a court of law."

"Or to Spain," Racine said. "She funded the voyage. Presumably she still holds legal title. Or to the Vatican, since it is religious in nature. I'm sure the government of the Bahamas will make a claim. The Mexicans will want it for their conquest collection in the anthropological museum. And then of course there's us. The United States will undoubtedly base its position on our discovery."

Roger was silent, still dazed, lost in his own thoughts, but Hilda nodded. She and Racine were scholars. Their duty was clear. They could wait. They were objective, removed from the message.

Mom was different.

"What we have here is Europe's gift to America." Her words were paced, calm, and I recognized the tone. It was her voice of preparation, the gathering of her forces. "What we have here was the promise, the pledge, the undiluted intent, the preconceived idea before any fact was known. This little nothing, this box anyone can lift, was the bond, was supposed to be a fair trade. And Columbus left it unopened. Never given. Never accepted."

Roger caught my eye. It took me a moment to tell what was different about him, but then I knew: he was listening. Usually when someone else was talking, Roger could hardly wait for them to stop so he could weigh in—agree or disagree, it didn't matter. He was always impatient for his turn to express an opinion, to argue his point of view. But not now. Now he was simply tuned in to Mom, as though he had something to learn.

While she was speaking, Mom reached across to Violet's car seat. My sister was awake now, a neutral observer as the voices tangled in the wind. She watched as Mom removed one clean diaper stored behind the cushion. She watched as slowly, deliberately, Mom wound it like a bandage around her stiff right hand.

"Europe got America, everything and everybody in it and on it, and in exchange we were supposed to take . . . this." Mom closed her eyes, concentrated her strength. Her next words were a whisper.

"We've waited long enough."

I saw the chop coming. Like every perfect movement in *dozen* it broke from nowhere and yet from everywhere at once. It arose from the inner self, from a long procession of subtle decisions, links in a fine chain, that finally translated into action. Mom *became* her white-wrapped hand and fell with it into the glass.

There must have been sound. Glass makes noise when it shatters on rock. But sometimes one sense overpowers all the others, blocks them out, and this time it was sight. Our eyes registered and recorded the event, not our ears.

There, framed by a halo of shards, was a twisted brown circle, a few pointed sticks.

There must have been sound. Five people breathing, a baby

at the end of her patience. And yet all was still. Even the wind seemed to pause, to draw into itself.

Like Cobb, I had expected jewels. Diamonds, rubies, emeralds. I had expected gold, the most valuable thing, the object that in and of itself was supposed to so dazzle the people Columbus found that they would welcome all those who came after.

"It was a crown after all," Mom said.

And it was a crown, no mistake. I recognized it from the picture over Grandma's bed: It was the Crown of Thorns.

AFTERWORD

Dreaming of Columbus

by

Gerald Vizenor

It is only fitting to give the final words in this book to a voice from Native America that is also, paradoxically, the voice of Columbus. In THE HEIRS OF COLUMBUS, *Gerald Vizenor brings us Stone Columbus, a crossblood trickster and heir of the discoverer. "The Maya created Columbus," Stone Columbus, wealthy proprietor of a bingo barge afloat in Lake of the Woods, announces on a radio talk show. Columbus "carried our tribal genes back to the headwaters of the great river, he was an adventurer in our blood and returned to his homeland."* THE HEIRS OF COLUMBUS *reflects the "new worlds and new words" of the encounter between two cultures, to use Vizenor's phrase. The novel is both wise and farcical, combining "ancient American storytelling with space-age literary techniques," in the words of Ishmael Reed.*

In this passage Stone Columbus dreams that he sailed with his namesake on the SANTA MARÍA, *arriving in the paradise of the islands. In Stone's dream the journals of Columbus mingle with the magical tale of how Columbus "lost his soul to a hand talker," Samana, an Indian woman, of how "he dreamed he traveled to the source of a great river." Columbus may have turned tribal culture to slavery, but "once he dreamed he was a child in our tribal world."*

As Americans we are the dreams and the nightmares of the dreams and the nightmares of Columbus.

Stone Columbus dreamed that he sailed on the *Santa María* that Sunday, October 28, 1492, into Bahia de Bariay. Samana danced with the blue puppets on the sterncastle as the flagship entered paradise. The water was deep and clear on the coast, and the broad leaves of the trees reached out to touch the ships near shore at the mouth of the river. The highest leaves wheeled in the lightest wind.

Samana rounded the decks with the puppets; her turns were sudden and silent, her breasts were golden, her thighs a wild radiance. The blue puppets chattered, golden birds bounced in the lower leaves, fish brushed the precious stones, and enormous brown flowers bloomed at dawn, but the dogs were silent and never barked. The tropical trees near shore held the blue shadows of the puppets, the living hollows of their creation.

"I have never seen anything so beautiful," Christopher Columbus wrote that night in his journal. "The country around the river is full of trees, beautiful and green and different from ours, each with flowers and its own kind of fruit. There are many birds of all sizes that sing very sweetly. . . . I took the small boat ashore and approached two houses that I thought belonged to fishermen. The people fled in fear. In one of the houses we found a dog that did not bark.

"It was such a great pleasure to see the verdure and those groves and the birds that it was hard to leave them. This island is the most beautiful I have seen, full of good harbors and deep rivers, and it appears that there is no tide because the grass on the beach reaches almost to the water."

Columbus lost his soul to a hand talker and puppets that night at Bahia de Bariay, the beauteous harbor and river he named San Salvador. The blue radiance of his birth and the stories in his blood were liberated at last in a burst of passion on the warm beach.

Samana danced once more in silence on the sterncastle. She wore a red cap, trade beads, and bells to tease the Admiral of the Ocean Sea. Her hands were wild, an immortal silence that burst in a blue radiance; the decks were blue, touchwood from the headwaters. The naked men on shore waved to the hand talker; two became puppets, and others were arboreal. Stone was blue in his dream and roamed in a white robe near the mangroves on the coast. The masts of the flagship and caravels were brushed by great golden birds. Samana brushed the decks; the sensuous rounds of her golden thighs bruised the memories of the tormented crew on the *Santa María*.

Columbus was overcome with pleasure, so touched and aroused that he was purblind to the crew and his mission for the first time in his life; nothing mattered that night but the golden thighs of the hand talker. He summoned the torment of his enormous penis, teased the carnal memories of his pained pleasures, but the hand talker healed him with pure lust and a vision of bears, panthers, and brown masters in the brush.

Samana dove from the sterncastle into the shadows at the mouth of the river, a blue radiant stream trailed her to the beach. Columbus removed his scarlet tunic and followed her in the water. That night he abandoned the curve of his pain in her hands and thighs and entered her maw to become a woman, a bear, a hand talker. His penis was hidden and blue, and his hair burned blue, the best stories in his blood. Samana vanished overnight in the New World.

Christopher Columbus wrote later in his survival letter that he dreamed he had traveled to the source of a great river. He watched his body, erect on the sterncastle the next day; his bones were lost on a mission, his soul scorned and abandoned with the histories of the Old World. In spirit he had returned to the headwaters of the great river in the New World.

"I weighed anchors this morning to sail westward from this harbor, in order to go to the city where according to the Indians the King dwells," he wrote in his journal on October 29. "After I went three miles I saw a river with a narrower entrance than the one at San Salvador. To this one I have given the name Rio de la Luna" in honor of his memories of Samana.

Morison wrote in *Admiral of the Ocean Sea* that the "Admiral prepared with pathetic punctilio an embassy to visit the Emperor of China. . . . The official interpreter Louis de Torres, a converted Jew 'who knew Hebrew and Aramaic and even some Arabic,' was made the head of it; and to him were intrusted all the diplomatic paraphernalia: Latin passport, Latin letter of Credence from Ferdinand and Isabella, and a royal gift, the nature of which unfortunately we do not know." Louis was told to return in six days.

Columbus was morose and more sullen by the night. His bones and memories ached for the hand talker; she had vanished without a trace but in his memories. Nothing but gold would ease his worries and a sense of spiritual separation.

Cruel and bitter ironies abound in the missions of wealth and Old World civilizations. Overnight his discoveries reduced tribal cultures to the status of slaves; at the same time the stories in his blood were liberated by a tribal hand talker.

"This day Martín Alonso Pinzón sailed away with the caravel *Pinta*, without my will or command," Columbus wrote on November 21. He was worried, unable to sleep, and his burdens became more serious with each day of the voyage.

Columbus returned a month later to the coast of Oriente Province near the Windward Passage. Once more he remembered the hand talker and the "sheer pleasure and delight" of her golden thighs. His memories of lust and paradise touched the entries in his journal on November 27; he wrote, "Yesterday at sunset I arrived in the vicinity of Cabo de Campana, but did not anchor even though the sky was clear and the wind light and there were five or six wonderful harbors to the leeward.

"Whenever I enter one of these harbors I am detained by sheer pleasure and delight as I see and marvel at the beauty and freshness of these countries, and I do not want to be delayed in pursuing what I am engaged upon. For all these reasons I stood off the coast last night and beat about until day."

The *Santa María* and the *Niña* remained at anchor in the harbor for six days because of rain and contrary winds. He waited for his luck to return, for a sign, but his troubles had only begun in the New World.

"At the hour of vespers we entered a harbor that I named Puerto de San Nicolás in honor of Saint Nicholas because it was his feast day," he wrote on December 6, from Hispaniola. Again, wind and rain delayed his voyage for several days.

Columbus wrote in his journal on December 24, "Among the many Indians who had come to the ship yesterday, telling us about gold on the island and where it could be found, was one who appeared to be bettered disposed and more friendly. I flattered him, and asked him to go with me to show me the gold mines." The colonial conceit of the gold hunt, even the first celebration in the New World of the birth and radiance of Jesus Christ, was overshadowed by a disaster on Christmas Day.

The *Santa María* was carried by the current and grounded on a coral reef in the Limonade Pass near Hispaniola. The rudder groaned and the seaward swells turned the flagship on the coral and the rocks punched holes in the wooden hull.

Columbus inherited the signature of survivance, discovered a new route to colonial wealth, and was responsible for one of the most notable shipwrecks in history. He concluded that the disaster was predestined, a sign of a wise leader. A tribal leader on the island would show the mariner how to discover gold; his directions would save the Old World mission and culture of death. Morison wrote in *Admiral of the Ocean Sea* that the tribal leader "presented to the Admiral, apparently without ironic intent, a great mask that had golden ears and eyes."

Columbus, determined to overmaster the disaster, wrote a convoluted interpretation in his journal on December 26: "I recognized that Our Lord had caused me to run aground at this place so that I might establish a settlement here. And so many things came to hand here that the disaster was a blessing in disguise. Certainly, if I had not run aground here, I would have kept out to sea without anchoring at this place because it is situated inside a large bay containing two or three bands of shoals."

Ferdinand Columbus, in *The Life of the Admiral*, wrote that his father forgot his grief over the loss of his ship when he was given gold. "God had allowed it to be wrecked in order that he should make a settlement and leave some Christians behind to trade and gather information about the country and its inhabitants, learning their language and entering into relations with the people."

The *Santa María* sank on a mission the tribes would never survive; the Old World lust for gold would silence tribal names and stories in a decade. "Those gold ornaments that seemed so abundant when the Spaniards first came," wrote Morison in *Admiral of the Ocean Sea*, "represented the labor and accumulation of several generations, the Indians' family plate as it were. By this time all had been stripped from the Indians. Gold could now be obtained only by washing it out of the sand and gravel in the beds of rivers and streams, or by a still more laborious process, possible only with directed slave labor. . . . Those who fled to the mountains were hunted with hounds and of those who escaped, starvation and disease took toll, whilst thousands of the poor creatures in desperation took cassava poison to end their miseries."

Christopher Columbus founded *La Villa de la Navidad* on Christmas Day, 1492, the first Old World settlement in the New World. He ordered a fort built on the beach, in honor of the disaster, with the remains of the *Santa María*. The thirty-nine sailors who were the first citizens of the settlement would not survive the year. "Before the shipwreck Columbus had no intention of founding a settlement on his voyage of discovery, for he had only enough men to work his vessels," wrote Morison. "Now, making a settlement answered the question what to do with *Santa María*'s people. There was no knowing what had become of *Pinta*, and the forty men from *Santa María* overcrowded little *Niña* with her crew of twenty-two."

Columbus had more trouble two weeks later; the first dangerous encounter with tribal people in the New World. The sailors attacked the tribe when they landed on the beach to gather supplies for the return voyage. "The sailors were ready, since I always advised my men to be on guard," he wrote in his journal.

"They gave one Indian a great cut on the buttocks and wounded another in the breast with an arrow."

The winter of their return from the New World was cold and the sea was tempestuous; the high and mighty waves crossed the bows of the flagship and caravels from two directions. The decks were beaten by cold water from the Old World and warm winds from the New World. Blue lights burst over the masts and sterncastles.

Columbus heard the blue storm puppets chatter for the last time on the deck. He remembered them near his home, at the convent, on the islands in the New World, and now he watched their graven images rise and beat with each wave, and he reasoned that their dance would balance the ships in the storm.

"Columbus was man enough to admit that he was as frightened as anyone," wrote Morison in *Admiral of the Ocean Sea*. "Jotting down his impressions of these terrible days of tempest, after *Niña* was safely anchored, he admitted that he should never have wavered as he did in trusting divine providence, which already had brought him safe through so many perils, and tribulations, and afforded him the glory of discovering a western route to the Indies. God must have intended that discovery to be of some use to the world."

Columbus worried to his death that his letter would be found at sea, and that he would be tried to defend his sanity over the stories of the storm puppets and a hand talker with golden thighs. "I sealed the parchment in a waxed cloth, tied it very securely, took a large wooden barrel, and placed the parchment in the barrel, without anyone knowing what it was . . . and had it thrown into the sea," he wrote in his journal.

Binn Columbus heard the stories in his letter, and other stories were told at the stone tavern. She heard the stories from his bones and ashes, his partial remains in a silver casket. "He died with lonesome memories," she told the heirs at the headwaters. "Once he dreamed that he was a child in our tribal world."

Samana conceived a daughter that blue night on the beach at Bahia de Bariay in Oriente Province. Samana was born the next summer at the stone tavern near the headwaters of the great river. Samana is a name that has been inherited for more than ten generations of hand talkers on the mount.

The soothsayer and the book. (ca. 1500)

TESTIMONIES

Contributors and Acknowledgments

Contributors are listed in the order of their first appearance. Sources cited or alluded to in the editors' introductions are also listed in order of appearance. Additional works, not cited in the text, are recommended here as well. This is a limited selection for beginning reading, and there are many excellent works we have failed to mention. Uncredited translations are by the editors; they are loose translations into a modern idiom, intended for the nonspecialist reader.

Foreword

ALASTAIR REID

New Yorker staff writer Alastair Reid set high standards for translation with his English versions of Neruda and Borges. Besides translations, his twenty-some books include poetry, children's books, and essays, including *Whereabouts: Notes on Being a Foreigner* (Berkeley: North Point, 1987). A considerably longer version of "Waiting for Columbus," which appeared in *The New Yorker* on 24 February 1992, drew further on Reid's experience and insight as a resident of the Dominican Republic.

INTRODUCTION:
The Myth of America

For Lévi-Strauss and the structuralist critics on the relation be-
tween myth and language, a good place to begin is three works
by Claude Lévi-Strauss: *Structuralist Anthropology* (New York:
Basic Books, 1963), *The Savage Mind* (Chicago: University of
Chicago Press, 1966), and *The Raw and the Cooked* (New York:
Harper & Row, 1970). Jacques Erhmann's *Structuralism* (Garden
City: Anchor Doubleday, 1970) is a fine introductory (but chal-
lenging) anthology containing excellent articles by Lévi-Strauss,
Todorov, and others. See also Umberto Eco's *A Theory of Semiotics*
(Bloomington: Indiana University Press, 1979), Fredric Jame-
son's *The Prison-House of Language* (Princeton: Princeton Univer-
sity Press, 1972), and Edmund Leach's *Genesis As Myth* (London:
Jonathan Cape, 1969). The quote from Humboldt appears in
Language and Myth (New York: Harper and Brothers, 1946) by
Ernst Cassirer, who is excellent on this subject.

FRANCISCO X. ALARCÓN

Alarcón (1954–   ) is the author of *Body in Flames/Cuerpo en
Llamas* (Francisco Aragon, trans., San Francisco: Chronicle
Books, 1990) and *Tattoos* (Oakland: Nomad Press, 1984). "Snake
Wheel" expresses the sense that the past endures in the present,
reflecting in part the cyclical view of time that prevailed in pre-
Columbian Mesoamerica. It is reprinted from Alarcón's *Snake
Poems: An Aztec Invocation* (San Francisco: Chronicle Books,
1992), in which the poet meditates upon a 1629 treatise on Aztec
beliefs compiled by his namesake, Hernando Ruiz de Alarcón, a
Mexican Catholic priest (1587–1646). The result of this unusual
collaboration (or confrontation) is a new work that draws its
power from the heritage of indigenous America.

Part One: Paradise

EDUARDO GALEANO

The three volumes of Eduardo Galeano's *Memory of Fire* trilogy are *Genesis, Faces and Masks*, and *Century of the Wind* (New York: Pantheon, 1985, 1987, 1988). Two earlier books available in English are *Open Veins of Latin America* and *Days and Nights of Love and War*. Born in Montevideo, Uruguay, in 1940, Galeano began his career as a political caricaturist for the socialist weekly *El Sol*. In 1973 he went into exile in Argentina and later lived in Spain, but has since returned to Uruguay. His most recent books are *The Book of Embraces* (New York: W. W. Norton, 1991) and *We Say No: Chronicles 1963–1991* (New York: Norton, 1992).

PETER MARTYR

Pietro Martire d'Anghiera, known as Peter Martyr, a skeptical and curious Italian cleric, wrote about the New World (which he never visited) in his *Decades of the Newe Worlde* (1555) which describes the early years of the Spanish Main with some thoroughness and for the most part with impressive discrimination. His account is available in a reprint of the 1885 *The First Three English Books on America* (New York: Kraus, 1971).

ULRICH SCHMIDT

Adventurers from all over Europe were lured by the gold and glory of the Americas. Schmidt's account is found in *The Conquest of the River Plate* (London: Hakluyt Society, 1891).

CARL ORTWIN SAUER

Despite the many biographies devoted to Columbus, we still find Carl Sauer's account of Columbus's activities in the Caribbean in *The Early Spanish Main* (Berkeley: University of California Press, 1966) the most illuminating. More than a biography of Columbus, this book provided one of the fullest and most sympathetic studies of the native cultures Columbus encountered, as well as an overview of subsequent developments along

■■■■■■■■■■■■■■■■■■■■■■■■■■■■■■■■■■■■■■

the mainland borders of the Caribbean. Sauer's *Sixteenth Century North America: The Land and the People as Seen by the Europeans* (Berkeley: University of California Press, 1971) is nearly as enlightening on the post-Columbian Northern Hemisphere. Sauer was a historical geographer of high scholarship, discriminating judgment, marked originality, and sharp opinion.

KIRKPATRICK SALE
A founder of the New York Green Party, codirector of the E. F. Schumacher Society, and a member of the board of the PEN American Center, Sale is the author of such books as *SDS*, *Power Shift*, and *Human Scale*. His *The Conquest of Paradise: Christopher Columbus and the Columbian Legacy* (New York: Knopf, 1990), which is both a biography of Columbus and an analysis of his impact on the Americas and of the evolving historical viewpoint toward him, has been criticized as an exercise in "Columbus bashing." Columbus's defenders argue that while Columbus's actions may be censureable by modern standards, in the context of his times he was no worse than most and better than many. Certainly Columbus was one of the more literate of the Spanish leaders, and many writers, such as Tzvetan Todorov, are persuaded that his religious sentiments were serious and genuine. Nonetheless, Columbus initiated and presided over one of the most destructive episodes in world history, and for this it is hard to excuse him. Sale's book is one of the best and most complete studies of Columbus that we know.

GIANNI GRANZOTTO
Granzotto's *Christopher Columbus: The Dream and the Obsession* (New York: Doubleday, 1985) is among the many recent works devoted to Columbus.

J. H. ELLIOTT
J. H. Elliott, Regius Professor of Modern History at the University of Oxford, has published numerous books and articles on late Medieval and early Renaissance Spain. Two of his articles,

"The Mental World of Hernán Cortés" which appeared in the *Transactions of the Royal Historical Society*, 17 (1967), and "The Discovery of America and the Discovery of Man," which appeared in the *Proceedings of the British Academy*, 17 (1967), are of particular interest; both were collected in *Spain and Its World 1500–1700* (New Haven: Yale University Press, 1989).

CHRISTOPHER COLUMBUS

Columbus needs no introduction. Long little more than a name (no picture of him exists), Columbus first became better known in the nineteenth century; his evolving reputation has been well charted by Kirkpatrick Sale in *The Conquest of Paradise*. The standard biography used to be Samuel Eliot Morison's rousing *Admiral of the Ocean Sea: A Life of Christopher Columbus* (Boston: Little, Brown, 1942). Morison is a Columbus apologist, and those who would like to see the navigator as a great man will find this biography the most satisfying, but we feel it has been supplanted by more recent works too numerous to enumerate. The best sources, we believe, may be Sale, Sauer, John Noble Wilford's balanced *The Mysterious History of Columbus: An Exploration of the Man, the Myth, the Legacy* (New York: Knopf, 1991), and Felipe Fernández-Armesto's level-headed *Columbus* (New York: Oxford University Press, 1991). One translation we have consulted in preparing our version of the excerpts from Columbus's log is Robert H. Fuson's *The Log of Christopher Columbus* (Camden, Maine: International Marine Publishing, 1987), but the best translation may prove to be John Cummins, *The Voyage of Christopher Columbus: Columbus's Own Journal of Discovery* (New York: St. Martin's, forthcoming and seen by us in a prepublication version), which also contains a good, brief (and generally sympathetic) portrait of Columbus. Other sources of Columbus's writings include *Journals and Other Documents* (New York: Heritage Press, 1963), *Select Documents Illustrating the Four Voyages of Columbus* (London, Hakluyt Society, 1930), *The Columbus Papers: the Barcelona Letter of 1493, the Landfall Controversy, and the Ludian Guides*, by Mauricio Obregón, Lucio Graves, trans.,

(New York: Macmillan, 1991), and Oliver Dunn and James E. Kelley Jr., trans., *The Diario of Christopher Columbus' First Voyage to America, 1492–1493* (Norman, Oklahoma: University of Oklahoma Press, 1989).

AMERIGO VESPUCCI

Vespucci (1451–1512), born in Florence, took part in several early voyages to the New World. Martin Waldseemüller, who published a German translation of Vespucci's *Mundus Novus* in 1507, proposed the New World be named America. This version was collected from volume five of the invaluable anthology edited by J. H. Parry and Robert G. Keith, *New Iberian World: A Documentary History of Latin America to the Early Seventeenth Century* (New York: Times Books, 1984).

EVAN S. CONNELL, JR.

The many books by Evan S. Connell, Jr. (1924–   ) include *The Connoisseur* (New York: Simon and Schuster, 1974), which tells of a man transformed by a pre-Columbian figurine, and *Son of the Morning Star: Custer and the Little Bighorn* (Berkeley: North Point, 1984). He lives in Santa Fe, New Mexico.

The introduction to these excerpts retells and simplifies Connell's account in "Vinland Vínland," part of *A Long Desire* (New York: Holt, Rinehardt & Winston, 1979); a companion volume is *The White Lantern* (New York: Holt, Rinehardt & Winston, 1980).

RALPH LANE

Lane (1530?–1603) came to Virginia in 1585. His account of his attempt to settle there was published in Hakluyt's *Voyages* in 1589. This selection was taken from Carl Sauer's *Sixteenth Century North America*.

HENRI JOUTEL

Joutel (1640–1735) is an important source of information on the voyages of the French explorer La Salle. This selection from Joutel's *Journal Historique* (in the Dépôt des Cartes, Plans, et Journaux de la Marine, Paris), was taken from *The Exploration of North America: 1630–1776* by W. P. Cumming, D. B. Quinn, and George Williams (New York: G. P. Putnam's Sons, 1974).

FRAY MARCOS DE NIZA

Fray Marcos (1495–1558) explored Arizona and New Mexico in 1539. His accounts of discovering the legendary city of Cíbola led to Coronado's arduous and fruitless exploration of the American Southwest, in which (following countless Americans) he discovered the Grand Canyon. This selection appeared in Sauer's *Sixteenth Century North America.*

ÁLVAR NÚÑEZ CABEZA DE VACA

Cabeza de Vaca (1490?–1557) was an Andalusian who came to America in 1527 in the service of Pámfilo de Narváez. He was stranded in Florida and spent ten years traversing the North American continent, finally arriving in Mexico. His *Adventures in the Unknown Interior of America* (Cyclone Covey, ed. and trans., Albuquerque: University of New Mexico Press, 1983) is one of history's great true adventures and a marvelous source of firsthand information about native North America.

GASPAR DE CARVAJAL

Carvajal (1504–64) was a priest of the Order of Santo Domingo de Cusman. His account of the discovery of the Amazon went unpublished until 1894. It was reprinted in J. Toribio Medina's *The Discovery of the Amazon According to the Account of Fray Gaspar de Carvajal and Other Documents* (B. T. Lee, trans. and H. C. Heaton, ed., New York: 1934).

MALCOLM MARGOLIN

Originally from Boston, Margolin graduated from Harvard College in 1962. He now lives in Berkeley, where he edits and publishes *News from Native America* and Heyday Books. This excerpt is from *The Ohlone Way: Indian Life in the San Francisco-Monterey Bay Area* (1978). *The Way We Lived: California Indian Reminiscences, Stories and Songs* (edited and with commentary by Margolin, 1981) is also published by Heyday Books.

ABEL POSSE

Born in Cordoba, Argentina, in 1936, Posse studied politics and literature in Paris and now lives in Buenos Aires. Long a member of the Argentine diplomatic service, Posse is the author of several novels, including the estimable *The Dogs of Paradise* (Margaret Sayers Peden, trans., New York: Atheneum, 1989), winner of the Romulo Gallegos Prize for the best novel written in Spanish over the previous five years, from which the excerpt is taken.

CHARLES OLSON

Influenced by historian Carl Sauer and literary mentor Edward Dahlberg, Olson (1910–70) developed an interest in the early history of America. In 1951, he lived in the Mexican Yucatán, where he studied Mayan culture. A 1991 biography by Tom Clark, *Charles Olson: The Allegory of a Poet's Life* (New York: W. W. Norton), resurrects the Olson personality. Olson's Maximus sequence was published in three volumes between 1960 and 1975 and collected in *The Maximus Poems* (George F. Butterick, ed., Berkeley: University of California Press, 1983).

Part Two: Gods and Demons

"For the Europeans, America was a marvel": on the rhetoric of the marvelous in European accounts of America, see Stephen Greenblatt's *Marvelous Possessions: The Wonder of the New World* (Chicago: University of Chicago Press, 1991). For native viewpoints on the conquest, Léon-Portilla's *The Broken Spears*, discussed below, is essential. (We are limiting ourselves to English-language texts here, but it is worth noting that there is considerable scholarly research available in Spanish from ethnologists and historians in Mexico and Central America in particular.) Gordon Brotherston's *Image of the New World: The American Continent Portrayed in Native Texts* (London: Thames and Hudson, 1979) is delightful and instructive and contains a wide range of texts not only in traditional alphabetical writing but also in pictograms and hieroglyphs in sandpaintings, wampum belts, pottery, and many other media of expression. Jerome Rothenberg's *Shaking the Pumpkin: Traditional Poetry of the Indian North Americans* (New York: Alfred van der Marck, 1986) is an excellent anthology, as is Peter Nabokov's *Native American Testimony* (New York: Viking, 1992). Robert Berkhofer, Jr.'s *The White Man's Indian* (New York: Random House, 1978) and Olivia Vlahos's *New World Beginnings: Indian Cultures in the Americas* (New York: Viking, 1970) are helpful. For contemporary Native American literary expression see *Harper's Anthology of 20th Century Native American Poetry* Duane Niatum, ed., (San Francisco: HarperSanFrancisco, 1978).

CHILAM BALAM

Parts of the *Chilam Balam*, the community books of the Yucatán Maya, are frequently quoted in a variety of translations, but the work as a whole is only now becoming available in excellent translations by Munro Edmundson, published by the University of Texas Press. A sense of the work can also be obtained from Spanish, French, and other English translations: *Libro de los libros de Chilam Balam* (Mexico: Fondo de Cultura, 1948); *Les Prophéties de Chilam Balam* (Paris: Gallimard, 1976); *The Book of Chilam Balam of Chumayel* (Norman: University of Oklahoma Press, 1967).

GERALD VIZENOR

Vizenor (1934–   ) teaches Native American literature at the University of California, Berkeley. His books include *Interior Landscapes: Autobiographical Myths and Metaphors* (Minneapolis: University of Minnesota Press, 1990), *Landfill Meditation: Crossblood Stories* (Hanover: Wesleyan University Press, 1991), and

Griever: An American Monkey King in China (Normal: Illinois State University, 1987), which won a Fiction Collective Prize and an American Book Award. The quotation cited in the introduction to this section is from the epilogue to his *The Heirs of Columbus* (Hanover: Wesleyan University Press, 1991), an excerpt from which appears as an afterword later in this volume. His most recent book is *Dead Voices* (Norman, Oklahoma: University of Oklahoma Press, 1992).

LESLIE MARMON SILKO

"I grew up at Laguna Pueblo [a reservation in New Mexico]," writes Leslie Marmon Silko. "I am of mixed-blood ancestry, but what I know is Laguna." Silko's books include a collection of letters with James Wright entitled *The Delicacy and Strength of Lace* (St. Paul: Graywolf, 1986) and the novel *Ceremony* (New York: Viking, 1977); her most recent novel is *Almanac of the Dead* (New York: Simon and Schuster, 1991). She is the recipient of a MacArthur Foundation grant. Her comments on her work quoted in the editors' introduction appeared in Jerome Rothenberg's *Shaking the Pumpkin*.

POPUL VUH

This translation, the most satisfying to us, is that of Munro Edmonson, in his *The Book of Counsel: The Popul Vuh of the Quiche Maya of Guatemala* (New Orleans: Tulane University Press, 1971); it was reprinted in Gordon Brotherston's *Image of the New World*. Another excellent translation is Dennis Tedlock, *Popul Vuh: The Definitive Edition of the Mayan Book of the Glories of Gods and Kings* (New York: Simon Schuster, 1985).

DIEGO DURÁN

Durán (1537?–1588) came to the New World from Spain as a young man. His *Historía de las Indias de Nueva España e Islas de la Tierra Firme* (Mexico: Purrua, 1967) is translated as *Book of the Gods and Rites and the Ancient Calendar* (Norman: University of Oklahoma Press, 1971) and (the final part, separate and abridged) as *The Aztecs: The History of the Indies of New Spain* (New York: Orion, 1964). Todorov, in *The Conquest of America*, calls him "one of the rare individuals who really understood both cultures— or, if you will, who is capable of translating the signs of the one into the signs of the other; thereby his work is the summit of six-teenth-century Spanish scholarship with regard to the Indians."

BERNARDINO DE SAHAGUN

Sahagún was born in Léon, Spain, in 1499. He sailed to Mexico in 1529, where he died in 1590. Sahagún's twelve-volume *General History of the Things of New Spain*, an anthropological and lin-guistic record of the Mexican people at the time of the conquest, is an extremely valuable work.

AZTEC: FLOWERS AND SONGS OF SORROW

Miguel Léon-Portilla's *Vicion de los Vencidos* (1959), published in an English translation by Lysander Kemp under the title *The Broken Spears: The Aztec Account of the Conquest of Mexico* (Boston: Beacon, 1962), is an indispensable compilation from extant native accounts, collected in "hope that this modest work will create further interest in the native accounts of the Conquest."

OCTAVIO PAZ

Winner of the 1990 Nobel Prize for Literature, the Jerusalem Prize, the Frankfurt Peace Prize, and the Neustadt Prize, Paz is the author of more than twenty-five books of poetry (mostly in fine translations by Eliot Weinberger) and prose. Born in 1914, he has worked in the Mexican diplomatic service in France and Japan, and was Mexican ambassador to India. Grove Weidenfeld recently issued an expanded (by more than double!) edition of Paz's classic 1961 work, *The Labyrinth of Solitude* (*The Labyrinth of Solitude and Other Writings*: New York, 1985).

B. TRAVEN

Traven, paradoxically, was famous for being unknown; he hid behind his pen name and kept his identity a closely guarded se-cret. Born around 1890, he seems to have spent his youth in Ger-many as an actor, an editor, and a revolutionary, and the greater part of his life, until his death, in Mexico. The outlines of his life have become clearer as a result of recent research, including at least three books: Will Wyatt's *The Man Who Was B. Traven* (London: Jonathan Cape, 1980); Judy Stone's *The Mystery of B. Traven* (Los Altos, Calif.: William Kaufmann, 1977), and Jonah Raskin's *My Search for B. Traven* (New York: Methuen, 1980). Less attention, unfortunately, has been paid to his large body of unique and highly accomplished fiction.

Part Three: Children and Cannibals

The best work on the fundamental attitudes assumed by the Europeans in their encounter with utterly alien peoples is Tzve-tan Todorov's *The Conquest of America: The Question of the Other* Richard Howard, trans., (New York: Harper & Row, 1982), dis-cussed below. See also Inga Clendinnen, "'Fierce and Unnatural Cruelty': Cortés and the Conquest of Mexico," which seems to be intimating that Todorov's approach suffers from cultural bias, as well as several other suggestive articles collected in *Rep-resentations 33: Special Issue, The New World* (Berkeley: University of California Press, Winter 1991).

CARLOS FUENTES

Between the publication of his first novel, *Where the Air Is Clear* (*La Region Más Transparente*, 1958; Sam Hileman, trans., New York: Farrar, Straus and Giroux, 1960), and *The Campaign* (Alfred Mac Adam, trans., New York: Farrar, Straus and Giroux, 1991), Carlos Fuentes, who was born in Mexico City in 1928, has published a large body of stories, novels, essays, and plays. The conquest of Mexico figures prominently in the play *All Cats Are Gray* and the novel *A Change of Skin* (New York: Farrar, Straus and

Giroux, 1967); the novel *Christopher Unborn*, Alfred Mac Adam and Carlos Fuentes, trans., (New York: Farrar, Straus, and Giroux, 1989) concerns a new Christopher born on the quincentenary of Columbus's arrival in the New World.

"Gabriel García Márquez and the Invention of America" was delivered as the second Allison Peers Lecture at the University of Liverpool, 13 March 1987, the same year in which Fuentes was awarded the prestigious Cervantes Prize, and was printed in *Myself with Others* (New York: Farrar, Straus and Giroux, 1988). Fuente's most recent work, *The Buried Mirror: Reflections of Spain and the New World* (New York: Houghton Mifflin, 1992) is a companion to his BBC television documentary on Hispanic culture.

JEAN RASPAIL

Raspail, author and explorer, has published some fifteen books in French. This selection is from *Who Will Remember the People . . .*, Jeremy Leggat, trans., (San Francisco: Mercury House, 1988); another Raspail novel recently published in English is *Blue Island* (San Francisco: Mercury House, 1991).

JUAN DE MATIENZO

The account of sixteenth-century Peru by Juan de Matienzo, who died in 1587, was finally published in Argentina in 1910, from the manuscript housed in the British Museum.

GARRISON KEILLOR

Born in Anoka, Minnesota, in 1942, Keillor is known for his radio broadcasts, *New Yorker* pieces, and such books as *Lake Wobegon Days* (New York: Viking, 1985), from which this excerpt is taken.

MICHEL DE MONTAIGNE

Montaigne (1533–92) wrote his *Essais* between 1571 and 1580. Our translation relies primarily on the version by E. J. Trechmann (New York: Oxford University Press, nd.).

ALEJO CARPENTIER

Carpentier (1904–80) combined interests in anthropology, history, and music. His oratorio *La Passion Noire* was first performed in Paris, where he studied and lived in the twenties and thirties. After the revolution in his native Cuba, Carpentier returned there from Venezuela, where he was living in exile, and became vice-president of the National Council of Culture and director of the Cuban State Publishing House. This selection is from *The Harp and the Shadow*, Thomas and Carol Christensen, trans., (San Francisco: Mercury House, 1990).

Part Four: Conquest

For the conquest as a biological exchange see Alfred W. Crosby's excellent *The Columbian Exchange: Biological and Cultural Consequences of 1492*. (Westport CT: Greenwood, 1973).

MICHELE DE CUNEO

Cuneo, who may have been a childhood friend of Columbus's, wrote a letter describing Columbus's second voyage in 1495; it was first published in 1885. Cuneo's letters to friends in Liguria (often quoted and available in many translations) are collected in the *Raccolta Columbiana de Genova;* one source of English translations is Columbus's *Journals and Other Documents*.

EDWARD DAHLBERG

Poet, novelist, essayist, and critic Dahlberg (1900–77) was born in Boston. His *Do These Bones Live* (New York: Harcourt, Brace, 1941), a volume of essays on American literature, was a particularly influential work. Dahlberg was Charles Olson's most important early mentor, although the two later quarreled. Arguing that "the more carefully we study history, the more important in our eyes will become the religious sense," Dahlberg impressed upon a generation of American writers the necessity of grounding literature in historical awareness. *The Gold of Ophir: Travels,*

Myths, and Legends in the New World (New York: E. P. Dutton, 1972) combines an original essay by Dahlberg with selections from Peter Martyr, Sahagún, and others.

THOMAS HARIOT

Hariot (1560–1621) wrote his *Briefe and True Report of the New Found Land of Virginia* in 1588. A facsimile edition, illustrated with twenty-eight engravings by Thèodor de Bry, is available from Dover Publications (New York, 1972).

GUILLERMO CABRERA INFANTE

Cabrera Infante (1929–   ), author of *Three Trapped Tigers*, Donald Gardner and Suzanne Jill Levine, trans., (New York: Harper & Row, 1981) and *Infante's Inferno*, Suzanne Jill Levine, trans., (New York: Harper & Row, 1984) as well as essays, movie reviews, and screenplays (such as *Vanishing Point*), was born in Gibara, Cuba. In 1954 he was jailed for publishing a short story with "English profanities." Cabrera was briefly head of the Council of Culture under Castro, but soon turned critical of his regime and has lived for the past twenty-five years in London. This selection is from *View of Dawn in the Tropics*, Suzanne Jill Levine, trans., (New York: Harper & Row, 1985).

CHIBCHA TUNDAMA

Tundama's speech was delivered in 1541. This selection, abbreviated from Lucas Fernández Piedrahita's *Noticia historial de las Conquistas del Nuevo Reino de Granada* (1688), appeared in Gordon Brotherston's *Image of the New World*. Ed Dorn collaborated with Brotherston in the English translation. Brotherston writes that "Tundama's own idea of peace . . . derived from the teaching of Bochica, the culture hero who by Chibcha reckoning visited [the region] in the first millennium B.C."

MICHAEL D. COE

Coe combined studies in literature and anthropology at Harvard College, where he took a doctorate in anthropology in 1959.

There are now many useful guides to the Maya and their culture and history, and subsequent scholarship has unearthed much information unavailable to Coe for his *The Maya* (London: Thames & Hudson, 1966). Still, *The Maya* remains an informative and readable overview. The translation of the passage from the *Chilam Balam* in "The Battle Flag Is Raised" is based on a version that appears in this book.

MIGUEL ÁNGEL ASTURIAS

Asturias (1899–1974) gained a reputation as a stylist with his *Leyendas de Guatemala* (1930), which reflected his studies of Mayan culture; he continued this interest in novels such as *Men of Maize* (G. Martin, trans., New York: Delacorte, 1975). Asturias was awarded the Nobel Prize for Literature in 1967. "Tecúm-Umán" appeared among the poems collected from 1943 to 1948 in *Poesia* (Argos-Buenos Aires: Sien de Alondra, 1949). We do not know of a previous translation.

SANDRA MESSINGER CYPESS

Cypess is a professor of romance languages and literatures at the State University of New York, Binghamton. Besides *La Malinche in Mexican Literature: From History to Myth* (Austin: University of Texas Press, 1991), she is the author of a number of critical articles, including scholarly articles on the role of La Malinche in the works of Elena Garro and Emilio Carballido. The quotations from Julie Greer Johnson (author of *Women in Colonial Spanish American Literature*, Westport, Conn.: Greenwood, 1983) and Adelaida R. Del Castillo (author of "Malintzín Tenépal: A Preliminary Look into a New Perspective," which appeared in *Essays on La Mujer*, Los Angeles: Chicano Studies Center, 1977) are both taken from *La Malinche in Mexican Literature*.

BERNAL DÍAZ DE CASTILLO

Bernal Díaz de Castillo (1492–81) recorded his experiences in the conquest of Mexico in his *Historía Verdadera de la Conquista de la Nueva España* (three volumes, 1632), written largely in response to the "authorized" account of Francisco López de Gómara, Cortés's chaplain. Díaz was an ordinary soldier and somewhat resentful of what he saw as Cortés's appropriation of the glory of the conquest from the troops. His account has an "eyewitness" flavor and is free from the formality and the literary embellishment of most contemporaneous works on the subject. It is vivid, personal, and dramatic.

HERNÁN CORTÉS

Cortés (1485–1547) first sailed to Santo Domingo in 1504. He was given command of a voyage of discovery in 1518, but to conquer Mexico he had first to defeat the official Spanish governor, Pánfilo de Narváez. No satisfactory biography is known to us, but J. H. Elliott's "The Mental World of Hernán Cortés," in *Spain and Its World* 1500–1700, is quite good, and Inga Clendinnen's " 'Fierce and Unnatural Cruelty': Cortés and the Conquest of Mexico" is interesting and helpful.

WILLIAM H. PRESCOTT

Prescott was born in Salem in 1796. His *History of the Conquest of Mexico* and *History of the Conquest of Peru* were published in 1843 and 1847 respectively, and are periodically in and out of print in reissue editions. Prescott died in 1859. A biography, *William H. Prescott*, by Donald G. Darnell, was published in 1975 (Boston: Twayne). His *Works*, in twenty-two volumes edited by Wilfred H. Munro and originally published in 1904, is again available from AMS Press (New York).

TRINH T. MINH-HA

Trinh T. Minh-ha is a Vietnamese-American filmmaker and the author of *Woman, Nature, Other: Writing Postcoloniality and Feminism* (Bloomington: Indiana University Press, 1989). For more on Trinh T. Minh-ha, as well as on changing perceptions of difference and of the relation of Self and Other as aspects of evolving artistic attitudes in a multicultural society, see Lucy R. Lippard's excellent illustrated *Mixed Blessings: New Art in a Multicultural*

America (New York: Pantheon, 1990). On the subject of multi-culturalism, see also *Multi-Cultural Literacy: Opening the American Mind*, Rich Simonson and Scott Walker, eds., (St. Paul: Graywolf, 1988), a literary anthology containing articles by Carlos Fuentes and Eduardo Galeano, among others.

TZVETAN TODOROV

Todorov, born in Sofia, Bulgaria, in 1939, is the author of (among other works) *The Fantastic: A Structural Approach to a Literary Genre* Richard Howard, trans., (Cleveland: Press of Case Western Reserve University, 1973) and *The Poetics of Prose* (Richard Howard, trans., Ithaca: Cornell University Press, 1977). He edited *French Literary Theory Today: A Reader* (Cambridge: Cambridge University Press, 1982). His thesis on the structures of signification in Choderlos de Laclos's *Dangerous Liaisons* was directed by Roland Barthes. The selection excerpted here is from *The Conquest of America: The Question of the Other* (Richard Howard, trans., New York: Harper & Row, 1982); another articulation of its themes can be found in *The Semiotic Conquest of America* (New Orleans: Graduate School of Tulane University, 1982).

WALT WHITMAN

"Prayer of Columbus" appeared in Whitman's *Two Rivulets* (1876). For the nineteenth-century Columbiana context, we are indebted to Kirkpatrick Sale's *The Conquest of Paradise*.

JIMMIE DURHAM

The selection is the title poem from Durham's collection *Columbus Day* (Minneapolis: West End, 1983). Durham, who was born in 1940, is also a sculptor and performer; for a good discussion of his work in these genres, see Lucy R. Lippard's *Mixed Blessings*. "We are not," Durham wrote in *We the People*, the catalogue of an exhibition of Native American art and video he curated with Jean Fisher, "part of your 'rich cultural heritage.' You did not inherit us or our history." In a broadside published for an exhibition of his work at the Orchard Garden, Derry, Northern Ireland, in 1988, Durham wrote that "as an authorized savage it is my custom and my job to attack." He now lives in Mexico.

Part Five: Mining Eden

The quotation from Columbus's log at the head of the editors' introduction to this section of the book has been rearranged by us in poetic form to emphasize its lyrical quality. Among the vast body of work relating to the exploitative post-Colombian American economy, Galeano's *Memory of Fire* is particularly instructive (and moving), and Sale's *The Conquest of Paradise* is also quite helpful. See also *Struggle and Survival in Colonial America*, David G. Sweet and Gary B. Nash, eds., (Berkeley: University of California Press, 1981) an anthology of twenty-one profiles of colonial Americans written for the nonspecialist but based on recent historical research. Rolando Mellafe's *Negro Slavery in Latin America* (Berkeley: University of California Press, 1975) and Leslie B. Rout Jr.'s *The African Experience in Spanish America* (Cambridge: Cambridge University Press, 1976) trace the history of blacks in colonial Latin America. A good literary treatment of the legacy of slavery from its American beginnings to modern times is João Ubaldo Ribeiro's monumental novel *An Invincible Memory* (New York: Harper & Row, 1989), a sweeping saga set in his native Bahia, Brazil. For North American slave narratives, see Henry Louis Gates, Jr., ed., *The Classic Slave Narratives* (New York, NAL/Dutton, 1987).

BARRY LOPEZ

Lopez is the author of the National Book Award-winning *Arctic Dreams: Imagination and Desire in a Northern Landscape* (New York: Scribner's, 1986), *Of Wolves and Men* (New York: Scribner's, 1979), *Crow and Weasel* (Berkeley: North Point Press, 1990), and several story collections. The quotation cited is from his lucid and eloquent *The Rediscovery of North America* (Lexington: University Press of Kentucky, 1991).

BARTOLOMÉ DE LAS CASAS

Bartolomé de Las Casas (1474–1566) was the first priest to be ordained in the New World (1510), and a champion of Indian rights. His *General History of the Indies*, not published until 1875, unleashed a flood of new information about Columbus and the early history of the West Indies.

FRAY ANTONIO DE MONTESINOS

Montesinos, who died in 1540, was one of a group of Dominican friars who arrived in the New World in 1510 and were soon appalled by the treatment of native peoples in the hands of the Spaniards. The group selected him to deliver the Advent Sunday sermon in 1511, advising the Spaniards that they were living in mortal sin. This sermon caused him to be recalled to Spain, where he lobbied for humane treatment of indigenous people, activity that, while it had little immediate effect, gave birth to protest in America. His story is told by Las Casas.

POPE PAUL III

Alessandro Farnese was pope from 1534 to 1549 (the period of the Council of Trent, 1545, and reformation in the face of Lutherian revolt). A patron of the arts, he commissioned Michelangelo's *Last Judgment*. Originally from *The Life of Bartholomew de Las Casas* by a Dominican father of New York (P. O'Shea, 1871), this excerpt was reprinted in Abel Plenn's interesting anthology *The Southern Americas: A New Chronicle* (New York: Creative Age, 1948).

JEAN FRANÇOIS GALAUP DE LA PÉROUSE

La Pérouse, a nobleman in France in 1741, was, as a young officer, taken prisoner by the English in the French and Indian War. More than two decades later he distinguished himself as an ally of the colonists in the American War of Independence and returned to France a hero. King Louis XVI then asked him to head a voyage of circumnavigation that would explore, in particular, unknown regions of the Pacific. After leaving papers and journals at various locations during his voyage, he died in a South Seas shipwreck. His papers were published in 1797 as *Voyage de La Pérouse autour du Mônde* ("The Voyage of La Pérouse Around the World"). The portion of this work pertaining to his visit to the Spanish mission at Monterey is available as *Monterey in 1786: The Journals of Jean François de La Pérouse* (Berkeley: Heyday Books, 1989). The selection from Malcolm Margolin describing conditions in the mission is from his introduction to this book.

EDWARD D. CASTILLO

Castillo is chairman of the Department of Native American Studies at Sonoma State University. His comments on conditions in the missions were published in "Mission Studies and the Columbian Quincentennial" in *News from Native America* (vol. 5, no. 4, summer 1991), in which he writes that "for Indians the Quincentennial will underscore the profound loss of our beloved homeland and the cruel dismemberment of our native cultures."

ALICE WALKER

Originally from Eatonton, Georgia, Walker, who was born in 1944, now lives in northern California. She won an American Book Award and Pulitzer Prize for *The Color Purple* (New York: Harcourt Brace Jovanovich, 1982). Besides novels, her many books include essays, short story collections, and poetry. *The Temple of My Familiar* (New York: Harcourt, Brace, Jovanovich) was published in 1989.

MICHAEL DORRIS & LOUISE ERDRICH

Michael Dorris, winner of the 1989 National Book Critics Circle Award for nonfiction and the Heartland Prize, is the author of *The Broken Cord* (New York: Harper & Row, 1989) and *A Yellow Raft in Blue Water* (New York: Henry Holt, 1987); books by Louise Erdrich, who won the National Book Critics Circle Award for fiction in 1984, include *The Beet Queen* (New York: Henry Holt, 1986) and *Tracks* (New York: Henry Holt, 1988). *The Crown of Columbus* (New York: Harper Collins) was published in 1991.

■■■■■■■■■■■■■■■■■■■■■■■■■■■■■■■■■■■■

INDEX

■■■■■■■■■■■■■■■■■■■■■■■■■■■■■■■■■■■■■■